# THE SIX
# SECRETS
# OF
# CHANGE

# THE SIX SECRETS OF CHANGE

What the Best Leaders Do to Help Their
Organizations Survive and Thrive

*Michael Fullan*

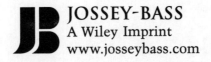

JOSSEY-BASS
A Wiley Imprint
www.josseybass.com

Published by Jossey-Bass
A Wiley Imprint
989 Market Street, San Francisco, CA 94103-1741—www.josseybass.com

Jossey-Bass books and products are available through most bookstores. To contact Jossey-Bass directly call our Customer Care Department within the U.S. at 800-956-7739, outside the U.S. at 317-572-3986, or fax 317-572-4002.

Jossey-Bass also publishes its books in a variety of electronic formats. Some content that appears in print may not be available in electronic books.

Credits appear on p. 153.

**Library of Congress Cataloging-in-Publication Data**

Fullan, Michael.
  The six secrets of change : what the best leaders do to help their organizations survive and thrive / Michael Fullan. — 1st ed.
    p.  cm.
  Includes bibliographical references and index.
  ISBN 978-0-7879-8882-1 (cloth); ISBN 978-1-1181-5260-7 (paper);
  ISBN 978-1-1181-1526-8 (ebk); ISBN 978-1-1181-1525-1 (ebk);
  ISBN 978-1-1181-1524-4 (ebk)
    1. Organizational change.  2. Communication in organizations.  3. Interpersonal communication.  4. Employee empowerment.  5. Employee motivation.  I. Title.
  HD58.8.F84 2008
  658.4'06—dc22

                                                                              2008000879

Printed in the United States of America

FIRST EDITION
HB Printing    10  9  8  7  6
PB Printing    10  9  8  7  6  5  4  3  2  1

# CONTENTS

# PREFACE

I HAVE WRITTEN ONE OTHER BOOK IN WHICH I DELIBERATELY examined an equal number of cases in the business and in the education literature to see what could be learned. What I found in 2001 was five powerful interrelated themes related to organizational success: moral purpose, understanding change, relationships, knowledge use, and coherence (Fullan, 2001).

Seven years and a million change stories later, I address this same question: What do we know about successful organizational change under complex conditions? Now we more urgently need answers to "the change question," and there is a lot to sort through. Just to name a few of the books on my desk: *The Eight Skills That Separate People Who Perform from Those Who Don't; The Three Tensions; The Five Minds of the Future; The Four Secrets of Long-Term Business Success and Failure; Seven Self-Destructive Habits; The Eight Essentials to Emotionally Connect Your Employees to Your Business; Twelve Elements of Great Managing.* Holy numerology!

My own six secrets have been gleaned from my work in understanding and bringing about large-scale, substantial change through education reform in England and Ontario (in both the public school system and in universities), as well as in engaging in major change initiatives around the world. The secrets have been tested in relation to the business literature, especially those studies that furnish data and name companies. The secrets enable us to view the lessons in the literature with a critical eye; they equip us with the capacity to discern what advice is likely to be on the right track and what advice is downright dangerous.

The six secrets are not secret in the sense that there is a conspiracy to hide them from public view; they are secrets because they are hard to grasp in their deep meaning and are extremely difficult to appreciate and act on in combination. The purpose of this book is to make the secrets accessible. I always strive in my writing to take critical change ideas of the day and make them (1) insightful, (2) actionable, and (3) concisely communicable. Moreover, the secrets travel well in both the private and the public sectors, as we will see in examples from a variety of businesses and from health and public education systems. Finally, they are especially apropos in the face of the complexities of the "flat world" characterized by Thomas Friedman (2005) and the even more complex "semiglobal" conditions detailed by Ghemawat (2007).

If you master the six secrets, you will approach change with newfound confidence reflecting Pfeffer and Sutton's elegant definition of wisdom: "the ability to act with knowledge, while doubting what you know" (2006, p. 174).

I will reveal what it takes to increase the chances of bringing about deep and lasting change. I will also show, as a few recent writers have, how misleading and dangerous it is to take the advice arising from seemingly successful organizations. Above all, the secrets guide you through the endemic uncertainties of change situations. If there were an answer to how to handle change, we would have found it long ago, and there wouldn't be a billion-dollar industry devoted to its pursuit. But there are approximations, and they are getting pretty damn good.

It is time to spread the secrets for everyone's good. Nothing is more important in the twenty-first century than learning to manage change. This book will help you do just that.

# ACKNOWLEDGMENTS

THE IDEAS BEHIND THE SIX SECRETS ARISE FROM MY WORK around the world in Australia, Chile, England, Hong Kong, Ireland, Malaysia, the Netherlands, New Zealand, Scandinavia, Scotland, South Korea, Thailand, the United States, Wales, and, of course, Canada. And the strategies are engaging all key players—politicians, government bureaucrats, members of the business community, parents, community leaders, students, teachers, administrative staff, and administrators. The ideas apply to the public and private sectors alike. I want to thank the numerous colleagues and friends who are working with me on this global agenda that is critical to our survival in the twenty-first century. I learn so much from them and from our work together.

A very special thanks to Premier Dalton McGuinty in Ontario. I have the privilege to serve as his special policy adviser, and we have had the opportunity to apply the secrets and learn from them in action in the public school system in Ontario from 2003 to 2007. Further, we have just been handed an overwhelming mandate from the electorate to go deeper in the next four years. When leaders do the right things, society benefits, and the strategy employing the Six Secrets works politically!

At home, Wendy and Conor provide a wonderful environment for living the good life. Not many people are as fortunate as I am, and I feel privileged on all fronts.

My thanks to Claudia Cuttress, who supported and shaped all the projects that fed into the secrets, and who helped produce this book—she is always a source of great ideas and invaluable support. I cannot thank her enough.

Finally, Jossey-Bass is the perfect publisher. Leslie Iura had the idea for this book and spurred me to write it. Matt Hoover and other editors were superb through the editing process to make the book stronger and better.

I thank all for allowing me to share our secrets. I hope you relish them.

# ABOUT THE AUTHOR

MICHAEL FULLAN IS PROFESSOR EMERITUS AT THE ONTARIO Institute for Studies in Education at the University of Toronto, and is special adviser on education to Dalton McGuinty, the premier of Ontario.

Fullan is a doer and thinker. He served as dean of the faculty of education at the University of Toronto from 1988 to 2003, leading two major organizational transformations, including a merger of two large schools of education. He is currently working as adviser and consultant on several major education reform initiatives around the world.

Fullan bases his work on research drawn from both the public and private sectors, finding an increasing convergence in the best of this literature. He has written several best-sellers that have been translated into many languages.

Visit his Web site at www.michaelfullan.ca.

Reactions to *The Six Secrets of Change* are welcome at changeforces@oise.utoronto.ca.

# THE SIX
# SECRETS
# OF
# CHANGE

# INTRODUCTION
## Have Theory, Will Travel

GIVE ME A GOOD THEORY OVER A STRATEGIC PLAN ANY DAY of the week. A plan is a tool—a piece of technology only as good as the mind-set using it. The mind-set is theory, flawed or otherwise. Theory is not abstract conjecture, and it is not about being cerebral. The biologist David Sloan Wilson (whose productive use of evolutionary theory we will take up later) captures the meaning best: "a theory is merely a way of organizing ideas that seems to make sense of the world" (2007, p. 16). Theories, in other words, make sense of the real world and are tested against it. The best theories are at their core solidly grounded in action.

Theories that travel well are those that practically and insightfully guide the understanding of complex situations and point to actions likely to be effective under the circumstances. Good theories travel across sectors of public and private organizations, and they apply to geographically and culturally diverse situations.

## Neither Theory nor Action

In his inimitably caustic manner, Henry Mintzberg (2004) dismantles the abstract theorizing taught in many MBA programs because it is theory out of context. As he puts it, "a *technique* might be defined as something that can be used in place of a brain" (p. 39, italics in original). Technique can be effective, but only "if applied with nuance by people immersed in a specific situation" (p. 39). Theories that travel are indeed laced with nuance.

MBA programs, concludes Mintzberg, are heavy on analysis, technique, and abstract strategy. But the question of effectiveness is not about how smart you are; it is about how *grounded and insightful* your theorizing is. And let us not forget that Enron, the most productive and scandalous megacompany of the 1990s, prided itself on its intellectual acumen. The leaders were "the smartest guys in the room" with the dumbest theory in action (McLean & Elkind, 2003). When describing Jeff Skilling, president and chief operating officer, and CEO for seven months in 2001 before Enron's implosion, McLean and Elkind report: "When people describe Skilling they don't just use the word 'smart'; they use phrases like 'incandescently brilliant' or 'the smartest person I ever met.' . . . He could process information and conceptualize new ideas with blazing speed. He could instantly simplify highly complex issues into a sparkling compelling image" (p. 28).

Enron flooded its executive ranks with MBAs, establishing a culture in which intellectual brawn and sheer brilliance were what mattered and what was rewarded lavishly. Designers, not diggers of ditches, according to McLean and Elkind. There are less egregious examples of theory gone bad than Enron, which we will refer to later in this introduction, but for now I will say that decontextualized ideas harbored in the best brains are not what I mean by theory that travels effectively.

If designing ditches is not enough, what about digging them? Action by itself is equally dangerous. Jack Welch, who had impressive success at GE over a twenty-year period from 1981 to 2001, represents a good example of why we should be wary of borrowing ideas from someone who has an underconceptualized theory. A close examination of his philosophy reveals the flaw in the action-only ointment, especially if the ideas are disseminated to others who lack Welch's forceful personality (come to think of it, *especially* when disseminated to dominant personalities: strong leaders with defective theories are particularly dangerous). Says Welch, "forget the arduous, intellectualized number crunching and data grinding that gurus say you have to go through to get strategy right. . . . In real life, strategy is actually straightforward. You pick a general direction and implement like hell" (2005, p. 165).

Welch's core strategy is called "differentiation" or the "vitality curve," which rates employees annually using three categories—A, B, and C (Welch, 2001, p. 159). The As are people "who are filled with passion and committed to making things happen"; the Bs "have good qualities but lack passion"; the C "is someone who can't get the job done." Once the employees have been categorized, Welch gets to work. "The As should be getting raises that are two or three times the sizes given to the Bs. Bs should get solid increases recognizing their contributions every year. Cs must get nothing" (p. 160).

Even if managers do not think they have any Cs, they are forced to employ the 20–70–10 rule. Usually the Cs are removed annually. You tell me whether this strategy has long legs or not. Is the automatic use of the 20–70–10 rule as it gets disseminated likely to create a climate of risk taking and trust, or will it erode effective action over time? We shall see that the vitality curve doesn't jibe with the six secrets, which in my view represent a theory that travels well. Authoritarian ideas in the business literature do travel; it is just that they travel dangerously.

Boudreau and Ramstad (2007, p. 13) report that between 2001 and 2003 "organizations spanning a vast array of sizes, industries, and maturities simultaneously adopted the 20–70–10 system." The logic of the spread of the 20–70–10 system was that if it worked for GE, why won't it work for us? (Incidentally, Enron used the 20–70–10 vitality curve.) Consider the hapless store manager on Fifth Avenue, New York, who had seen Welch interviewed on television the night before and wanted to ask a follow-up question. As Welch proudly recounts, "The store manager brought me to a secluded section, under a staircase where no one could hear us. He explained that he had 20 people in his sales force. 'Mr. Welch,' he asked, 'Do I really have to let two go?' 'You probably do if you want to have the best sales staff on Fifth Avenue'" (2001, p. 434).

Have theory, will unravel!

Jack Welch had a lot of good leadership qualities; what he didn't have was a theory that travels. I have deliberately chosen a "successful" case—GE, the market cap of which Welch helped build by more than $400 billion (but beware of what Sheth [2007] refers to as "volume obsession," a self-destructive habit)—to show how dangerous it is to adopt the surface techniques of successful companies. You need a much better compass than one provided by a single technique; there are no good shortcuts.

Mintzberg (2004) similarly questions the long-term efficacy of another of GE's favorite techniques, the "workout." Workouts begin with a presentation by a manager, who issues a challenge or problem and then leaves. As Welch describes it, for the next two or three days, "without the boss present and with no facilitator to grease the discussions, employees were asked to list problems, debate solutions, and be prepared to sell their ideas when the boss returned" (2001, p. 182). Not a bad idea, but it is a technique without an underpinning theory. Action learning is good, but it must be accompanied by reflective insight tied to an underlying theory that guides further action. Techniques by themselves are just tools.

Mintzberg acknowledges that Welch was right to worry about excessive bureaucracy at GE—the reluctance to take action—but wonders about the purpose of "action learning." He makes this incisive observation: "Do managers need more action, or greater opportunity to reflect on the more-than-enough action they already have? Put differently, do they need to enhance their capacity to reflect on the action they already take?" (p. 227).

Mintzberg furnishes his own conclusion: "Learning is not doing; it is reflecting on doing" (p. 228). He also states that "there may be something instinctive about managing but it has to be learned too, not just by doing it but by being able to gain conceptual insight *while* doing it" (p. 200; italics in original). The six secrets are precisely suited to reflection-in-action. Now we are getting closer to a theory that will travel.

## One Big Caution

*B*efore getting to the actual theory, there is one overriding caution: *the world has become too complex for any theory to have certainty.* There can never be a blueprint or silver bullet. Never take what you read (even the six secrets) at face value. Robert Rubin, who spent eight years in the Clinton administration, put it best: "Once you've internalized the concept that you can't prove anything in absolute terms, life becomes all the more about odds, chances, and trade-offs. In a world without provable truths, the only way to refine the probabilities that remain is through greater knowledge and understanding" (2003, p. 57).

If you want complexity, try Thomas Homer-Dixon's *The Upside of Down: Catastrophe, Creativity and the Renewal of Civilization* (2006). Homer-Dixon describes five "tectonic stresses": population stress, energy stress, environmental stress (land, water, forests, fisheries), climate stress, and economic stress (the ever-widening income gap between rich and poor people). He carefully shows how these stresses are likely to have multiplier effects leading to "synchronous failure." We will have something to say about passion, moral purpose, and happiness in later chapters, but for now I can say that mastering the six secrets puts leaders in a position to act with greater purpose and conviction, though always keeping in mind the wise proviso that they must "act with knowledge while doubting what [they] know" (Pfeffer & Sutton, 2006, p. 174).

It may seem odd that in this book I am giving you advice and then cautioning you to doubt it, but that is precisely what I am doing. Probably the two greatest failures of leaders are indecisiveness in times of urgent need for action and dead certainty that they are right in times of complexity. In either case, leaders are vulnerable to silver bullets—in the one case grasping them, and in the other, relishing them.

Rosenzweig (2007) gives us plenty of reasons (nine to be exact) why we should be wary of drawing management advice from even the most successful cases. He cites nine business delusions that deceive managers. The foremost delusion is the halo effect, which is the "tendency to make inferences about specific traits based on a general [and retrospective] impression" (p. 50); that is, once an organization is seen to be successful, people attribute its success to traits evidenced in the organization *after the fact*. As Rosenzweig documents, for every trait you identify in a given successful organization, you can find the opposite trait in another successful organization (for example, *stick with your core business* versus *diversify to find new opportunities*). Thus the halo effect makes it unwise to adopt uncritically GE's vitality curve or workout.

Referring to psychological experiments, Rosenzweig demonstrates that "once people—whether outside observers or participants—believe the outcome is good, they tend to make positive attributions about the decision process" [or other characteristics of the organization] (2007, p. 34). In other words, ex post facto explorations are suspect if you are only examining cases of the already successful. Another delusion Rosenzweig discusses is the mistaking of correlation for causality. The traditional example is the mistaken conclusion that the greater the number of storks in an area, the higher the birthrate (real reason: the birthrate used to be higher in rural areas, where storks tend to be more common). A third delusion is that of single explanations. My current favorite is that Finland has the highest literacy performance in the world, and does not have national tests; ergo, other countries should eliminate national tests. There's no need to dwell on the remaining six delusions, but they add up to a clear warning to be cautious about books that generalize from the practices of already successful organizations. Collins's famous *Good to Great* (which we will return to later) suffers the same fate; according to Rosenzweig (2007), "If you start by selecting companies based on outcomes, and then gather data by conducting retrospective interviews and collecting articles from the business press, you're not likely to discover what led some companies to become *Great*. You'll mainly catch the glow from the Halo effect" (p. 120).

Basically, Rosenzweig is saying that success in a complex world is unpredictable because of uncertain customer demand, unpredictable competitors, changing technology, and a host of other vagaries. Instead of looking for certainties in the business literature, "Managers would do better to understand that business success is relative, not absolute, and that competitive advantage demands calculated risks. To accept that few companies achieve lasting success, and that those who do are best understood as having strung together several short-term successes rather than having consciously pursued enduring greatness" (2007, p. 158).

I recommend traveling with a good theory because theories never assume absolute certainty and are humble in the face of the future. Good leaders are thoughtful managers who use their theory of action (such as the six secrets) to govern what they do while being open to surprises or new data that direct further action.

## Theories That Travel

One example of a good theory that travels is evolutionary theory—the idea that plants, animals, and humankind adapt to changing environments over time. Evolutionary theory predicts and finds that long-term evolution favors ever-expanding boundaries of cooperative behavior, but not under all circumstances—such as when the environment is hostile.

It is not my purpose to examine evolutionary theory per se, but Wilson demonstrates what a good theory can do as he has applied it to various studies of animals and human beings, including studies of altruistic behavior and religion.

Another example of good theory that travels and one closer to the substance of our interests comes from my good friend Michael Barber (2007), former head of Tony Blair's Prime Minister's Delivery Unit (PMDU). Barber's theory of action includes ambitious goals, sharp focus, clarity and transparency of data, and a relentless sense of urgency. In terms of operations, he talks about (1) precise targeting of goals and resources; (2) incentives for developing new capacities, especially with respect to those people or organizations not doing well; (3) alternative providers; (4) prescription in demanding that all providers gather data, identify best practices, apply them, and be held to account; (5) empowered customers, and (6) checking, checking, and checking that programs are being implemented effectively.

PMDU focuses on making significant improvements in the following areas (Barber, 2007, p. 50):

| Health | Heart disease mortality |
| | Cancer mortality |
| | Waiting lists |
| | Waiting times |
| | Accident and emergency |
| Education | Literacy and numeracy at age eleven |
| | Math and English at age fourteen |
| | Completion of five advanced subjects |
| | in secondary school |
| | Truancy |

| Home office | Overall crime and breakdown by type |
| | Likelihood of being a victim |
| | Offenders brought to justice |
| Transport | Road congestion |
| | Rail punctuality |

Now there is an agenda for which one needs a theory that travels well! Barber and his colleagues—more accurately leaders and workers in the four sectors—did achieve improvements in all areas, sometimes going from awful to adequate, and other times from awful or adequate to good. Impressive, given the scope and scale—societal improvement in a country with over sixty million people. Still, the results are only adequate to good, so the Barber theory of action needs more refinement and better implementation, as he himself would agree.

My point is not to endorse Barber's particular theory, but rather to illustrate what I mean by a theory of action, one well grounded in applied problem areas, up for scrutiny in terms of the strategies themselves and, of course, the strategies' intended and unintended consequences.

We can now look at the six secrets. Figure I.1 illustrates the set.

There are five assumptions and criteria that underpin the set. First, the theory is meant to apply to *large-scale reform*. The goal is to change whole organizations, whole systems. In my own current work, for example, this includes improving the entire public school system of Ontario. Second, the set has to be understood as *synergistic*—each of the six feeds on the other five. Third, they are *heavily nuanced*—that is, it takes a lot of thought and application to appreciate their meaning and use. Fourth, they are *motivationally embedded*, by which I mean that one of the main reasons the theory works is that the six

Figure I.1: The Six Secrets

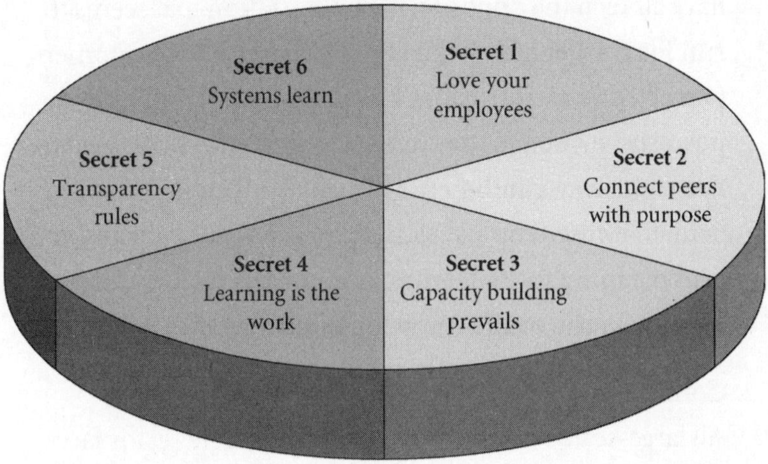

components serve to motivate the vast majority of people to invest the passion and energy needed to get results—what I sometimes call mobilizing a million change agents. Fifth, each of the six represents a *tension or dilemma*, which means you can err in one direction or another—the sophisticated leader holds them in dynamic tension. Every secret requires dynamic balance, or what Roger Martin calls *The Opposable Mind* (2007). For example, you don't choose between loving your employees *or* your customers; you do both in an integrated fashion. In Secret Two, you don't emphasize top-down or bottom-up strategies; you blend them. And so on. I will discuss the Opposable Mind further in Chapter Six.

Let's introduce the secrets briefly here and then go into them in depth in the next six chapters.

1. Love your employees.
   If you build your organization by focusing on your customers without making the same careful commitment

to your employees, you won't succeed for long. And we have all seen the opposite: the organization that seems to run for the benefit of the employees, with the customer perceived as an intrusion. Neither will do. I will provide powerful evidence that investing in your employees in the right way can be enormously profitable. The key is in enabling employees to learn continuously and to find meaning in their work and in their relationship to coworkers and to the company as a whole.

2. Connect peers with purpose.

All large-scale reform in the public or private sector faces what I call the too tight–too loose dilemma. If you want large-scale reform, you had better focus and tighten the requirements; but if you go too far, people feel constrained, and rebel. At the same time, local people need to be empowered. But if you devolve power and resources to local entities—the "let a thousand flowers bloom" approach—you get uneven results. (A thousand flowers do not in fact bloom, and those that do are not perennial!) I will show, with plenty of concrete examples, that the solution to this dilemma comes from the top, but not directly. It comes from leaders who embed strategies that foster continuous and *purposeful peer interaction*. The social glue of simultaneously tight-loose systems will stick, not when rank-and-file workers fall in love with the hierarchy—those in charge at the top—but rather when they fall in love with their peers. The job of leaders is to provide good direction while pursuing its implementation through purposeful peer interaction and learning in relation to results.

3. Capacity building prevails.

Capacity building entails leaders investing in the development of individual and collaborative efficacy of a whole group or system to accomplish significant improvements. In particular, capacity consists of new competencies, new resources (time, ideas, expertise), and new motivation. Many theories of action use fear and punitive accountability. I will maintain that this gets at best short-term and fleeting results. Bullying back-fires when it comes to complex change. The opposite of such approaches—nonjudgmentalism—doesn't mean that you avoid identifying things as effective or ineffec-tive. Rather it means that you do not do so pejoratively. Put another way, there are better ways to instill fear than through negative judgment—for example, by combining transparency and peer interaction. Pejorative judgments have their place, as when someone is abusive or engaged in criminal and fraudulent acts, but as motivators they need to be used sparingly. The main gains will come from the six secrets in concert, none of which contains blatant judgmentalism.

4. Learning is the work.

One of my Australian colleagues wrote a paper with the wonderful title "Professional Development: A Great Way to Avoid Change" (Cole, 2004). In other words, there is far too much going to workshops, taking short courses, and the like, and far too little learning while doing the work. Learning external to the job can represent a use-ful input, but if it is not in balance and in concert with learning in the setting in which you work, the learning will end up being superficial. I will present evidence that effective organizations see working and learning to work better as one and the same.

5. Transparency rules.

By transparency I mean clear and continuous display of results, and clear and continuous access to practice (what is being done to get the results). Transparency can be abused, such as when results are used punitively, but there is no way that continuous improvement can occur without constant transparency fueled by good data. When this secret is implemented in combination with the other five, the gains far outweigh the costs. Besides, transparency is here to stay in the flat world of the twenty-first century. When transparency is consistently evident, it creates an aura of "positive pressure"—pressure that is experienced as fair and reasonable, pressure that is actionable in that it points to solutions, and pressure that ultimately is inescapable.

6. Systems learn.

Systems can learn on a continuous basis. The synergistic result of the previous five secrets in action is tantamount to a system that learns from itself. Two dominant change forces are unleashed and constantly cultivated: knowledge and commitment. People learn new things all the time, and their sense of meaning and their motivation are continually stimulated and deepened. As we shall see, learning also means being humble in the face of complexity.

# Using a Good Theory

*Y*ou can use the six secrets directly to guide and monitor your leadership and organization. Or you can use them to screen managerial advice from the business literature, as I did with Jack Welch and GE. Or if you applied the criteria of the secrets to organizations in their heyday, you would worry sooner than was the case with Enron, which was named the most innovative company in the world by *Fortune* for six straight years in the 1990s. Yes, I am in danger of falling victim to the halo effect (or perhaps the devil's horn effect)—attributing causes once I know the outcome—but Enron leaders were not team players and valued neither their employees nor their customers. Time wounds all heels.

You can also use the six secrets to preempt the development of bad habits, such as the seven self-destructive habits of good companies, outlined by Sheth (2007): denial, arrogance, complacency, competency dependence, competitive myopia, volume obsession, and the territorial impulse. These befell such companies as Digital, IBM, Intel, Xerox, A&P, and General Motors. Once a self-destructive habit exists, it is difficult to overcome, primarily because it is an addiction. Sheth's direct advice is to address the bad habit rationally. For example, to break the habit of denial, he recommends the following steps: look for it, admit it, assess it, and change it. Rational advice to address an emotional problem is unlikely to help. Instead, and Sheth takes this very position in his final chapter, one should take steps to prevent the development of bad habits in the first place. He has a number of suggestions relative to the seven bad habits, but my position is that the six secrets contain built-in mechanisms that serve as positive checks and balances that inhibit the growth of bad habits.

Good theories are critical because they give you a handle on the underlying reason (really the underlying thinking) behind actions and their consequences. Without a good theory, all you can do is acquire techniques—surface manifestations of the underlying real McCoy. Recognition of this truth, incidentally, is one of the reasons why Toyota doesn't mind sharing its practices (Liker, 2004). You can borrow or steal a technique, but never a philosophy or culture.

The six secrets together form a strong theory that can help you sort through the gurus' advice. They point the way as you interpret ideas and situations and assess advice in the business literature. In *Hard Facts, Dangerous Half-Truths and Total Nonsense,* Pfeffer and Sutton (2006) say that you have to do three things in considering ideas from external sources. (1) Is the success you observe brought about by the practice you seek to emulate? (This relates to Rosenzweig's halo effect.) (2) Why is a particular practice linked to performance improvement? "If you can't explain the underlying logic or theory or why something should enhance performance, you are likely engaging in superstitious learning and may be copying something that is irrelevant or even damaging." (3) What are the downsides and disadvantages of the practice, even if it is a good one? In other words, have a good theory to guide your decisions and actions.

I would also advise that you bring an independent mind to any business books recommending their brand of solution (including this one). I myself always take a critical eye to any business (or education) books that recommend solutions with certainty. This caveat is reinforced by Rosenzweig (2007) and by Micklethwait and Wooldridge's irreverent *The Witch Doctors: Making Sense of Management Gurus* (1996).

Micklethwait and Wooldridge put it this way: "Management theory . . . has four defects: it is constitutionally incapable of self-criticism; its terminology usually confuses rather than educates; it rarely rises above common sense; and it is faddish and bedeviled by contradictions" (p. 12).

Concerning their first point, I have read hundreds of management books and have come across only three written by insiders who are critical of the field (Mintzberg, 2004; Pfeffer & Sutton, 2006; and Rosenzweig, 2007), and one written by outsiders—two editorial writers from the *Economist* (Micklethwait & Wooldridge, 1996).

On the question of fads and contradiction, Micklethwait and Wooldridge quote one manager: "In the past 18 months we have heard that profit is more important than revenue, quality is more important than profit, that people are more important than profit, that customers are more important than our people, that big customers are more important than our small customers, and that growth is key to our success" (p. 60).

The message, then, is don't believe everything you read, including books on management and, of course, including the six secrets. *Caveat lector* (no, not Hannibal's brother, but Latin for "reader beware"). Look for the argument and the evidence behind the claims. Go deep in trying to understand the meaning of my advice. Develop your own theory of action by constantly testing it against situations and ideas. Test the six secrets against your own experiences and intuition.

Riddle: When is a revealed secret still a secret? Answer: When it is heavily nuanced. We need to go much deeper into the content and specifics of each secret in action to appreciate their meaning. This is the task of Chapters One through Six.

## SECRET ONE
## Love Your Employees

### ·SECRET TWO·
### Connect Peers with Purpose

### ·SECRET THREE·
### Capacity Building Prevails

### ·SECRET FOUR·
### Learning Is the Work

### ·SECRET FIVE·
### Transparency Rules

### ·SECRET SIX·
### Systems Learn

# SECRET ' ONE

# Love Your Employees

*T*heories can be very general or more grounded. For our purposes—helping leaders thrive in complex times—theories need to be close to the action. Secret One takes us all the way back to the general theory of Douglas McGregor a half century ago. McGregor (1960) contrasted two theories of human motivation concerning behavior in the workplace, which he called Theory X and Theory Y.

### Theory X Assumptions

- The average human being has an inherent dislike of work and will avoid it if he or she can.

- Because of their dislike for work, most people must be controlled and threatened before they will work hard enough.

- The average human prefers to be directed, dislikes responsibility, is unambiguous, and desires security above everything else.

### Theory Y Assumptions

- If a job is satisfying, then the result will be commitment to the organization.

- The average person learns under proper conditions not only to accept but to seek responsibility.

- Imagination, creativity, and ingenuity can be used to solve work problems by a large number of employees.

Let's go back even further to Frederick Taylor, a proponent of Theory X almost a century ago in his *Principles of Scientific Management* (1911/2007). According to Taylor's studies in the steel industry, work tasks could be broken down, and workers could be taught to perform them with maximum efficiency and productivity. Taylor (2007) developed four principles of scientific management:

1. Replace rule-of-thumb work methods with methods based on a scientific study of the tasks.

2. Scientifically select, train, and develop each worker rather than passively leaving them to train themselves.

3. Cooperate with the workers to ensure that the scientifically developed methods are followed.

4. Divide work nearly equally between managers and workers, so that the managers apply scientific management principles to planning the work, and workers actually perform the tasks [p. 31].

Taylor demonstrated, for example, how a worker could be taught to nearly quadruple the volume of pig iron he moved simply through optimal timing of lifting and resting. (Incidentally, the six secrets actually integrate Theories X and Y and even Taylor's principles, but we are getting ahead of ourselves.) We leave Taylor for the time being and return to his ideas on the more modern concepts of precision and specificity. We will see that there is no incompatibility between being consistent in using what we know while being open to improvements (Secret Four).

Taylor did discuss the relationship between managers and workers, and this goes to the heart of secret one. We need here to examine more closely the relationship between employees and customers, and how managers conceive of this relationship. To take an education example, consider what looks like a straightforward case: that children should be first. Secret One belies that one-sided conclusion.

The major trumpet call for education in the United States is a piece of legislation called *No Child Left Behind*. England's is *Every Child Matters*. New York City's is *Children First;* these are the first two sentences of its report: "We call our plan Children First and we mean it. Our goal is to focus everything we do on the only outcome that matters: student success" (New York City Department of Education, 2007, p. 1).

I have centered my own work around the moral imperative of raising the bar and closing the gap of achievement for all children, so I am an advocate of the sentiments expressed in these policies. But there is one problem: Secret One tells me that the children-first stances are misleading and incomplete.

A new report from McKinsey and Company focusing on the top-performing school systems in the world provides the central reason why we must value employees (in this case teachers) as much as customers (children and parents): "the quality of the education system cannot exceed the quality of its teachers" (Barber & Mourshed, 2007, p. 8). I'll mention two examples of how even the best school superintendents can miss the nuance of Secret One, knocking its delicate balance out of whack. Gerry

House was superintendent of the Memphis City School District in Tennessee from 1992 to 2000. The Memphis district has 110,000 students and 161 schools. One in three children live in poverty. The superintendent's theory of education was to commit the district's schools to select among seven so-called whole-school reform models that had been sponsored by a national agency.

By 1998, 75 of the 161 schools were involved, with more being added. House was awarded the 1999 National Superintendent of the Year Award. Yet within a year she resigned. What went wrong? The answer is very much Secret One foretold in a 1998 report by an external research team: "teachers and principals express fatigue and feel unappreciated" (cited in Franceschini, 2002). Superintendent House, in the heat of battle in 1999, responded to teacher protest saying that "lagging test scores in city schools leave no room for the faint-hearted." (Any time you hear a manager say that the work is not for the faint-hearted, head for the exit, because this is a sure sign that Secret One is not understood.)

A similar example of another great school superintendent concerns Tony Alvarado, the highly successful leader of District 2 in New York City, who moved in 1997 to become chancellor of instruction (reporting to chief superintendent Alan Bersin) in the San Diego Unified School District. Alvarado and Bersin were in a moral hurry, as well they should have been, considering the low performance scores of students in San Diego schools. The relentless push from the top was met with mounting resistance in the union and on the part of some teachers. Alvarado was asked to leave in 2002, and Bersin was replaced by the school board in early 2005. The story is complicated (see Hubbard, Mehan, & Stein, 2006), but my point is that Bersin and Alvarado never figured out how to love their employees as much as their customers (students and parents). And yes, if you must choose one over the other, choose your customers, but my point is that this approach is doomed to failure.

Carl Cohn, who replaced Bersin as superintendent, publicly distanced himself from the Bersin-Alvarado approach and wrote an article in the national publication *Education Week* titled "Empowering Those at the Bottom Beats Punishing Them from the Top" (2007). Shades of Secret Three, but not the nuances; it is not just that you don't punish them, but also that you invest in their capacity building linked to results.

Secret One, then, is not just about caring for employees. It is also about what works to get results. It is about sound strategies linked to impressive outcomes. One of the ways you love your employees is by creating the conditions for them to succeed. This notion is related to George Bernard Shaw's observation: "the difference between a flower girl and a lady is not how she behaves, but how she's treated." This is pure Theory Y. But there is more to it than that. It is helping all employees find meaning, increased skill development, and personal satisfaction in making contributions that *simultaneously* fulfill their own goals and the goals of the organization (the needs of the customers expressed in achievement terms). If that fulfillment is not simultaneous for employees and customers, Secret One is not in place. In implementing Secret One, you can have your Theory X and eat your Theory Y too.

# Secret One in Action

One of my criteria for theories that travel is that they help us make sense of the world while guiding action in a good way. The test of Secret One is whether there is any proof that loving employees and customers equally can be done such that everyone benefits. I have already made the point that one without the other is deficient, but what does combining them look like, and what proof is there that the results are beneficial?

I find solid evidence in a book with the cute title *Firms of Endearment* (Sisodia, Wolfe, & Sheth, 2007). The fact that it is grounded in evidence relative to named companies is especially helpful. Firms of endearment (FoEs), say Sisodia et al., endear themselves to stakeholders (customers, employees, investors, partners, and society). When these authors claim up front that *no stakeholder is more important than any other*, they are getting at the core of Secret One. FoEs create emotional value, experiential value, social value, and financial value. Customers, the authors say, "want to be in love, and if they don't find it, they'll settle for price and convenience" (p. 5). We will get to their full list of companies shortly, but let's look for a moment at Wal-Mart (not an FoE) and Target (an FoE). Wal-Mart treats its employees instrumentally at best and offers low prices and convenience. Customers can be loyal in behavior to a company without being loyal in attitude: they might frequent a store because of low prices, but have no emotional attachment and therefore little long-term commitment to it. Any competitor that values quality and treats the customer well, as we shall see, will outperform other companies in the long run. As Sisodia et al. put it, "the logical 'left brain' says you should shop at Wal-Mart so that your shopping ends up saving a few bucks. However, the emotional right brain may not welcome the experience. Integrating the two sides is one of the secrets to Target's success [whose] customers get low prices, as well as a pleasant experience and more stylish products than they could find at Wal-Mart" (p. 5).

If you want bottom line, consider that Wal-Mart's stock has been stagnant for five years, whereas Target's has risen nearly 150 percent.

Companies that do not understand Secret One do not prosper as much as those that do. I have already predicted that General Electric would be in trouble with its tough approach. GE was renowned for its pragmatic, hard-nosed management and its record of earnings improvements (Sisodia et al., p. 8). GE's stock is down 40 percent over the past five years. It is relevant to compare the two rivals who were in contention to replace Welch. Jeff Immelt, who was appointed CEO, is more of an FoE leader and is trying to reinvent GE along those lines. Immelt is "a cooler, humbler and more reserved chief executive" than Mr. Welch, observes the *New York Times* ("Is GE too big for its own good?" 2007, p. B1), and quotes Immelt: "We have to re-earn the respect of investors."

Sisodia et al. (2007) also quote Immelt:

The reason people come to work for GE is that they want to be about something that is bigger than themselves. People want to work hard, they want to get promoted, and they want to get stock options. But they also want to work for a company that makes a difference, a company that is doing great things in the world. Good leaders give back. The era we live in belongs to those who believe in themselves but are focused on the needs of others. . . . The world's changed. Businesses today aren't admired. Size is not respected. There's a bigger gulf today between the haves and have-nots than ever before. It's up to us to use our platform to be a good citizen. Because not only is it a nice thing to do, it's a business imperative [pp. 31–32].

The GE senior executive who lost out to Immelt was Robert Nardelli—more in line with GE's tradition under Welch (and in fact was known as "Little Jack"). Nardelli was then immediately appointed as CEO of Home Depot in December 2000. Erring on the too-tight side of the equation, Nardelli streamlined operations and centralized supply orders, which resulted in the doubling of sales. Revenue increased from $45.7 billion in 2000 to $81.5 billion in 2005. (Incidentally, this was a slower rate of growth than Home Depot had previously experienced—the company had doubled in size every four years from 1979 to 2001, admittedly largely through expansion.) The cracks began to show as employees and customers were turned off by Nardelli's hard, results-driven management and as the company's share price eventually stagnated. Nardelli abruptly resigned in January 3, 2007, with a severance package of $210 million, which further alienated stakeholders. On August 5, 2007, as I write this chapter, it was announced that Nardelli has been appointed as chairman and CEO of Chrysler. Watch out, Chrysler, unless Nardelli has learned more about Secret One through his experiences at Home Depot. (Irony of ironies, business guru Ram Charan, 2007, p. 102, lavishes ten pages of praise on Nardelli for his leadership at Home Depot in "reinventing an entire social system." Caveat lector.)

I am aware that this analysis runs the risk of attributing the ups and downs of a company to the CEO as the dominant figure. In fact, as I will conclude eventually, it is the *culture* of the entire organization that counts, shaped by the CEO but manifested by leaders at all levels of the organization.

Sisodia et al. (2007) did not begin their selection process by assessing companies' financial performance. (In other words, they avoided the halo effect by deferring the question of success.) Instead, in their first stage they sought nominations of companies that met their "humanistic performance" criterion—that is, they looked for companies that paid equal attention to all five stakeholders (customers, employees, investors, partners, society). They then proceeded to an initial screening (stage two), to in-depth research of the companies that passed screening (stage three), and to final selection of the FoEs (stage four). The following are the twenty-eight companies that made the final cut (p. 16):

| | | | |
|---|---|---|---|
| Amazon | eBay | Johnson & | Southwest |
| BMW | Google | Johnson | Starbucks |
| Carmax | Harley | Jordan's | Timberland |
| Caterpillar | Davidson | Furniture | Toyota |
| Commerce Bank | Honda | LL Bean | Trader Joe's |
| Container | IDEO | New Balance | UPS |
| Store | IKEA | Patagonia | Wegmans |
| Costco | JetBlue | REI | Whole Foods |

Now we can work backwards. What was the financial performance of the companies in absolute terms and relative to their competitors? What did these companies stand for and do to get such results? First, let's look at the results of the financial analysis. Based on S&P 500 performance over the ten-year period between 1996 and 2006, "*the public FoEs returned 1,026 percent for investors over the 10 years . . . compared to 122 percent for the S&P 500; that's more than an 8-to-1 ratio!* (Sisodia et al., 2007, p. iv; italics in original).

Sisodia and his colleagues then made a direct comparison with Jim Collins's eleven *Good to Great* (2001) companies (Abbott,

Circuit City, Fannie Mae, Gillette, Kimberly-Clark, Kroger, Nucor, Philip Morris, Pitney Bowes, Walgreens, and Wells Fargo):

- Over a ten-year horizon, FoEs outperformed the *Good to Great* companies: 1,026 percent return versus 331 percent (a 3-to-1 ratio).

- Over five years, FoEs returned 128 percent, compared to 77 percent by the *Good to Great* companies (a 1.7-to-1 ratio).

- Over three years, FoEs performed on par with the *Good to Great* companies: 73 percent to 75 percent.

None of the eleven *Good to Great* companies made the cut as an FoE (although Gillette came close). Put differently, none of the *Good to Great* companies met the "humanistic performance" criteria.

In a nutshell, Secret One concerns the involvement of every-one in a company in meaningful pursuits that transcend the bottom line. Much of the detailed analysis of the cultures of FoEs feeds into several of our subsequent secrets, and I will make the connections at the appropriate times. But now let's con-sider one set of comparisons in the food industry: Whole Foods, Albertsons, Kroger (one of the *Good to Great* companies), Safeway, Costco, and Wal-Mart. Whole Foods' declaration of independence states that, among other things, "satisfying all of our stakeholders and achieving our standards is our goal. One of the most impor-tant responsibilities of Whole Foods' leadership is to make sure the interests, desires and needs of our various stakeholders is kept in balance. We recognize that this is a dynamic process. It requires participation and communication by all our stakeholders" (Sisodia et al., 2007, p. 128).

Whole Foods generated a 185 percent return to investors in the past three years and 400 percent over the past five years, when the S&P 500 rose by only 13 percent. Kroger (the *Good to Great* company) lost over half its value from 1999 to 2006, when the stock sat at around 45 percent of its 1999 value.

Another puzzle: How can FoEs provide higher wages and better compensation to employees while having lower overall labor costs? Answer: they have less turnover (which is financially beneficial) and greater productivity.

Costco, Wegmans, and Trader Joe's are good cases in point:

> They offer outstanding wages to their employees and competitive prices to their customers—and make healthy profits to boot. The higher wages and benefits paid by these companies do not show up in prices consumers pay. The greater productivity of higher-caliber employees and lower employee turnover in part explains this. Also, employee-generated process improvements continuously show up because employees care enough to continuously strive to make the company more profitable. Finally, the link between satisfied employees and customer loyalty is beyond question. These companies and FoEs in general do better in getting a share of wallet by a far greater focus on share of heart than is customary in their industry. Talk about alchemy. Higher wages and benefits transmuted into lower operating costs [Sisodia et al., 2007, p. 243]!

In-depth case studies by other business researchers of FoEs corroborate Sisodia et al.'s findings. Gittell's study (2003) of Southwest

Airlines is a fine example. With all the ups and downs in the airline industry—fuel cost crises, 9/11 and its aftermath—Southwest has had thirty-three consecutive years of profit and has never engaged in employee layoffs. On all measures—costs per seat-mile, aircraft productivity (hours in use), and labor productivity—Southwest consistently outperforms American Airlines, Continental, Delta, Northwest, United, and US Airways. Gittell identifies Southwest's "secret ingredient" (as she calls it) as "its ability to build and sustain high performance relationships among managers, employees, unions, and suppliers" (p. xi). She delineates ten synergistic Southwest practices for building high-performance relationships, which happen to cut across the six secrets: lead with credibility and caring, invest in frontline leadership, hire and retain for relational competence, use conflicts to build relationships, bridge the work-family divide, create boundary spanners, measure performance broadly, keep jobs flexible at the boundaries, make unions your partners, and build relationships with suppliers (p. 55).

Toyota, another of Sisodia et al.'s FoEs, has been even more carefully documented (Liker, 2004; Liker & Meier, 2007). I will save my discussion of Toyota for other chapters, but the company's investment in employees and its integration of Theory X (precision) and Theory Y (motivating employees) stand out as prime examples of the secrets at work.

A study of Canada's "best-managed companies" contains many of the same themes (Grnak, Hughes, & Hunter, 2006). The companies featured are Magnotta Winery, Spin Master, Boston Pizza (nothing to do with Boston—founded by two Greek immigrants in Edmonton who thought Boston sounded worldly), EllisDon, Harry Rosen, Armour Transportation Systems, Mediagrif Interactive Technologies, PCL Construction Group of Companies, Cirque du Soleil, and National Leasing. The success of all of these companies is predicated on attracting and investing in high-performing employees who provide superior service through innovation and commitment to their peers, to customers, and to the companies themselves.

An early example of a company that knew Secret One but lost it is Xerox. Joe Wilson, the creator of Xerox, was a prototypical example of a leader who instinctively operated from a Secret One basis, thereby changing the world of photocopying in the 1960s (Ellis, 2006). Wilson helped build Xerox from a fledgling nonentity called Haloid in the late 1940s. It was renamed Haloid-Xerox in 1958 and became Xerox shortly after. By 1965, Xerox's revenue was over $500 million; it was the world's leading photocopier company within a decade. (How many of us still refer generically to "Xeroxing" a copy?). Wilson, who died in 1971, carried a little card in his wallet that said, "to be a whole man, to attain serenity through the creation of a family life of uncommon richness, through leadership of a business which brings happiness to its workers, serves well its customers and brings prosperity to its owners; by aiding a society threatened by fratricidal division to gain unity" (quoted in Ellis, p. ix). The original firm of endearment! Wilson's sentiments, unpopular in the business world in the 1960s, aided and abetted him through the years of struggle in establishing Xerox during that time.

Ellis comments, "While casual observers may celebrate Wilson's astounding financial success, his real achievement as a leader and manager were in his rigorous financial discipline, his focus in developing a new technology, and his remarkable capacity to keep his organization committed to his vision for many long, lean years while going through the uncertainties of deliberate transformation change" (2006, p. 80).

Back in 1948, when addressing Haloid employees, Wilson said, "We want you to be proud of Haloid. We want your job to excite you, to make you feel that you're a person of dignity, a part of a valuable creative effort. With it all we want you to enjoy it here and to take pride in your work. . . . [We want] to create the kind of organizational morale that will be the envy of others . . . and Haloid will be a model of the kind of business that our country needs" (quoted in Ellis, 2006, p. 10).

Wilson understood that financial rewards were important but secondary to "value delivered to customers and society combined with career satisfaction and personal fulfillment of many individual people" (Ellis, 2006, p. 237). Wilson stepped down as CEO in 1968, and his secret to success was lost on his successors. Xerox went into decline for the next two decades or more, and has only been back on track since the turn of the century.

The principle of valuing employees as well as customers is equally if not more important in the public sector. When the newly elected Liberal government came to power in October 2003, I had the opportunity to begin work with Premier Dalton McGuinty as his special adviser on education (a post I still hold, as the government has been re-elected for another four years, from 2007 to 2011), allowing us to pursue the six secrets in action by improving Ontario's education system. For the past four years, we have designed and implemented a strategy to significantly improve a public school system that was in a rut. Ontario's student achievement in reading, writing, and mathematics was flat-lined in the previous five-year period from 1998 to 2003. During that same period, members of the government and the teaching profession were engaged in exercises of mutual acrimony and disrespect. Our new policy was based on a strong commitment to respect the teaching profession and invest in teachers' development, with an equal focus on results. In other words, we respected our employees as well as our customers. In the years 2004 to 2007, we have had steady growth in literacy and numeracy achievement in grades 3 and 6, as assessed by the independent provincial agency (the Education Quality and Accountability Office), improving some 10 percent or more in reading, writing, and mathematics across the whole system. Much more work remains to be done to make Ontario's education system great, so we will need to deepen our six secrets theory and persist with its implementation.

We have two indirect indicators in Ontario of the impact of Secret One. The number of new teachers to leave the profession in the first three years has declined—in the period 2003–2006, the percentage of teachers leaving in their first three years of teaching (the 2003 graduating cohort of seven thousand) was 7.5 percent, compared to figures ranging between 22 and 33 percent in the 1990s (based on three-year cohort samples; McIntyre, 2006). At the other end of the scale, the number of teachers retiring on full pension at first opportunity (typically age fifty-five) has declined. In 2006, there were some fifteen hundred fewer teachers retiring at this stage compared to the 1990s. We can't directly calculate the impact of the motivation of new and veteran teachers alike to put in the effort to improve the public school system, but there is no doubt that the system is healthier and more productive. Secret One at work.

## Secret One in Perspective

First, it turns out that Secret One is more encompassing than its simple wording implies. Yes, it is about employees and customers and their symbiotic connection. But it also includes three other parties, as Sisodia et al. (2007), Joe Wilson, and others point out: investors or shareholders, partners (suppliers, retailers, and even competitors), and society. As we study the six secrets, we will see more clearly that the five stakeholder groups and their prosperity are intimately related. Nevertheless, I won't change the wording of the secret—loving and investing in your employees in relation to a high-quality purpose is the bedrock of success.

Second, I believe that the nuanced meaning of Secret One allows you to distinguish between management books that contain superficial advice about the importance of employees and those that go deeper. Such books as *Brand from the Inside: Eight Essentials to Emotionally Connect Your Employees to Your Business* (Sartain & Schumann, 2006) and *Growing Great Employees: Turning Ordinary People into Extraordinary Performers* (Andersen, 2006) strike me as excessively instrumental compared to what I recognize as deeply connected books that treat employees, customers, and other stakeholders as truly equal, such as Sisodia et al.'s *Firms of Endearment* (2007), Liker's *The Toyota Way* (2004; and Liker & Meier, 2007), and Morrell and Capparell's fine treatment (2001) of the leadership lessons from the great Antarctic explorer Sir Ernest Shackleton (whom we will encounter in the Conclusion). When Morrell and Capparell describe his actions and observe that "Shackleton always put the well-being of his crew first" (p. 37), you believe it deep down—cognitively and emotionally. At least my theory tells me so.

Secret One is strongly corroborated in Sirota, Mischkind, & Meltzer's (2005) comprehensive study of *The Enthusiastic Employee*. Based on years of research with millions of employees, Sirota et al. document the power of three factors in motivating employees—fair treatment, enabling achievement, and camaraderie. They show that when these three components are experienced by employees they become highly engaged in work, service to customers is valued, and profits increase. Only 13.8 percent of all the organizations they surveyed could be classified as having an "enthusiastic workforce" (75 percent of employees rating the company high on all three dimensions). Secret One allows us to appreciate Sirota et al.'s findings, but the six secrets in total point to what is missing. It is true that camaraderie touches on our Secret Two (connect peers with purpose), but we see little in Sirota of transparency, capacity building, and leadership development more generally. We get an incomplete version of what is necessary to be a great organization.

Third, Secret One is perhaps the foundation secret, but in any case the six are deeply interrelated and in some cases overlapping, in the sense that the same action can enhance several secrets simultaneously. The six do operate to reinforce each other, and in this sense the task of implementing the secrets becomes easier as you begin to get multiple payoffs.

One of the most vexing problems in large systems concerns the need for cohesion of otherwise loosely coupled components. What is the right glue? How do you address the too tight–too loose dilemma that plagues most large organizations? Secret Two provides the answers.

·SECRET ONE·
## Love Your Employees

## SECRET TWO
## **Connect Peers with Purpose**

·SECRET THREE·
## Capacity Building Prevails

·SECRET FOUR·
## Learning Is the Work

·SECRET FIVE·
## Transparency Rules

·SECRET SIX·
## Systems Learn

# SECRET · TWO

# Connect Peers with Purpose

*A* serious problem that large systems face, one that becomes more perplexing in an ever more complex, diverse world, is how to achieve a degree of cohesion and focus in an otherwise fragmented environment. In earlier chapters, I've referred to this as the too tight–too loose dilemma. Focus the organization with sharp goals and tight accountability, and you get passive or alienated workers. Go for decentralized creativity, and you get drift and inertia. The key to achieving a simultaneously tight-loose organization lies more in *purposeful peer interaction* than in top-down direction from the hierarchy. This is Secret Two. The nuance is that connecting peers with purpose does not require less leadership at the top, but rather more—more of a different kind.

## The Conditions and Value of Peer Interaction

*A* nother analyst who found a theory that travels well is Thomas Friedman (2005), who unlocked a torrent of ideas when he formulated a framework based on the idea that the social world is flat. Conditions in the flat world empower individuals and groups to collaborate and compete globally.

Friedman identifies three forces that have converged to create lateral conditions. The first is technology, the global web that "enabled multiple forms of collaboration—sharing of knowledge and work—in real time, without regard to geography, distance or, in the near future, even language" (2005, p. 126). The second factor involves new ways of doing business in which managers and freelancers take advantage of the new flatter playing field to develop "horizontal collaboration and value-creation processes and habits" (p. 178). The third factor is the increasing participation of three billion people previously excluded from the playing field—those in China, India, Russia, Eastern Europe, Latin America, and Asia.

New technology, new habits of collaboration, and hordes of new players. A lot can go wrong when these unstoppable forces are unleashed. And this is precisely why we need new leaders versed in the nuances of the six secrets: "A crisis is a terrible thing to waste!" (Paul Romer, quoted in Friedman, 2005, p. 306).

Thus, current conditions are more conducive to peer or lateral interaction. Individuals leading organizations into global marketplaces will need more than Friedman's metaphor. This is not a book on global strategy, so I will offer the reader a caution and an excellent resource. The world is not really flat in the sense that differences don't matter. In a detailed analysis, Ghemawat (2007) furnishes convincing evidence that the world is really "semiglobal," because differences still matter a great deal depending on the goal and industry. He offers a useful CAGE distance framework for measuring the degree of differences along "cultural, administrative, geographic, and economic dimensions" (p. 34) that any organization should employ as a strategy tool if it is involved in or contemplating expanding into the global arena. For our purposes here, I am more interested in peer interaction within the organization and with peers in other units or branches within the company.

Let's start with the role and importance of peer interaction. I love the story that Wilson (2007), our evolutionary theory friend from Chapter One, tells: "According to legend, William James [the famous psychologist] was once approached after a lecture by an elderly woman who shared her theory that the earth is supported on the back of a giant turtle. Gently, James asked her what the turtle was standing upon. 'A second far larger turtle!' she replied confidently. 'But what does the second turtle stand upon?' James continued, hoping to reveal the absurdity of her argument. The old lady crowed triumphantly, "'It's no use, Mr. James—it's turtles all the way down!'" (p. 133).

As Wilson says, it's groups all the way down. In his view it is groups that matter, for better for worse. I say, show me a cohesive, creative organization, and I'll show you peer interaction all the way down.

Wilson also reports on a practical experiment by a poultry scientist named William Muir. Muir wanted to increase egg production by selective breeding and tried to do so in two ways. In modern egg production, hens live in groups (typically nine or so) in cages. In the first method, Muir selected the most productive hen from each of a number of cages; in the second method, he selected all the hens from the most productive cages (some of which, of course, were not as productive as the hens in the first method). After six generations, Muir reported his findings.

He first showed a slide of the sixth generation of hens selected by the first method: "The audience gasped. Inside the cage were only three hens, not nine, because the other six hens had been murdered. The three survivors had plucked each other during their incessant attacks and were now nearly featherless" (Wilson, 2007, p. 34). In other words, the most productive hens achieved their success by suppressing the productivity of their cage mates.

Then Muir shared a slide of hens selected from the second method: "The cage contained all nine hens, plump and fully feathered. . . . Egg production had increased dramatically during the course of the experiment. By selecting whole groups, [Muir] had selected against aggressive traits and for cooperative traits that enabled hens to coexist harmoniously" (Wilson, 2007, p. 34).

People differ from hens in at least one distinct way: they can feel and think. They can use these abilities for good or evil. The six secrets contain the ingredients for good—good values, good results. As I use the term here, *good values* refer to moral purpose, striving to develop oneself, and make a meaningful contribution through one's work and life—a concept that cuts across the secrets and is addressed more explicitly in the Conclusion. To serve this purpose, the values in question must be realized in actions that obtain results.

We can readily recognize the evil end of the continuum, such as aggressive individuals pushing to win at all costs, like our boys and girls at Enron. Clearly, working in groups in and of itself is not the answer because of the possible closed-mindedness of *groupthink,* a term coined by Irving Janis (1982) that describes "a mode of thinking that people engage in when they are deeply involved in a cohesive in-group, when the members' striving for unanimity overrides their motivation to realistically appraise alternate courses of action" (quoted in Wilson, 2007, p. 202). The Bay of Pigs, the *Challenger* space disaster, Hitler, and terrorist groups come immediately to mind. Groupthink is too tight; pure individualism is too loose.

Purposeful peer interaction, or perhaps I should say *positive* purposeful peer interaction, works effectively under three conditions: (1) when the larger values of the organization and those of individuals and groups mesh; (2) when information and knowledge about effective practices are widely and openly shared; and (3) when monitoring mechanisms are in place to detect and address ineffective actions while also identifying and consolidating effective practices. Okay, these points are too abstract and won't travel well, but we can be more specific.

In *Mavericks at Work: Why the Most Original Minds in Business Win*, Taylor and LaBarre (2006), in a manner akin to Sisodia et al. (2007), identify effective practices (similar to the six secrets) using named companies. Maverick companies look for ideas with a higher calling (What values does your company stand for? What purpose does your company serve?). They select and cultivate people who can find meaning and are seeking experiences that contribute to their own development and fulfillment. And they use the group—peer interaction—to get smarter and to achieve unusually better results. We meet the FoE Whole Foods again. The company has developed a business approach that "blends a taste for libertarian politics, a commitment to selling healthy foods and ensuring the compassionate treatment of animals, an eagerness to share financial information and decision-making authority up and down the organization, and a true zest for growth" (Taylor & LaBarre, 2006, p. 56).

As Taylor and LaBarre put it, "what is it about the ideas your company stands for, its point of view in the market-place, the ways in which employees interact with customers or collaborate with one another that becomes irresistible to the best people in your industry?" (p. 197). Put another way, Secret Two is about how organizations engage peers in purposeful interaction where quality experiences and results are central to the work.

More fully to the point of this chapter (the social glue) is the philosophy of SEI investments in Oaks, Pennsylvania, as expressed by Al West, the CEO: "Because we do all of our work in teams, working together is more important than managing up. When people don't get ahead here, it's not because of their boss, it's because of their peers. People who are always making sure their boss sees them, who direct their efforts up the chain rather than to their colleagues, are the ones who don't work out. Your success here is a direct function of how well you get along with your peers. . . . The problem with hierarchies is that they require you to engineer everything in advance" (quoted in Taylor & LaBarre, 2006, pp. 239–240).

The power of purposeful peer interaction is also captured in Surowiecki's *The Wisdom of Crowds* (2004). In complex, flat-world times, purposeful groups do better than a handful of experts, but you have to work the group. There has to be a sense of purpose, freedom from groupthink, consideration of diverse ideas, and retention of practices that work.

All these authors show that when problems or conditions are complex—which is surely true for businesses and public sector leaders today—purposeful peers are more effective. Peers are more effective than random individuals at work and more effective than managerial groups at the top working by themselves to develop strategic plans.

I and others have used Secret Two to good advantage in moving systems forward in the face of complex challenges. After England had its initial success in improving literacy and numeracy across the country in 1997–2001, results plateaued for three years in a row. One of the strategies that enabled school leaders to transcend the plateau was a primary school initiative in which the government funded fifteen hundred groups of six schools each to learn from each other about how to move literacy forward. This covered almost one-half of the primary schools in the country. This strategy had all the ingredients of using the wisdom of the crowd. It has common purpose (improving literacy in the country); there were good ideas out there (stimulated by the capacity building that occurred in the 1997–2001 period); and it used peer interaction to influence the spread of effective practices.

The use of peer interaction as social and intellectual glue has its roots within collaborative organizations, but it is much more than mere collaboration. Our own strategies endorse and facilitate intraschool collaboration, in which teachers learn from each other—what some researchers call professional learning communities—but now we have initiatives in which schools learn from each other (as when schools work in clusters or when urban schools are twinned). We even have strategies in place where school districts learn from each other. We call this lateral capacity building, and there are a growing number of examples of this approach from around the world.

In Ontario, the Literacy and Numeracy Secretariat has established two powerful examples of lateral capacity building. One is called the Ontario Focused Intervention Partnership, in which some 1,100 lower-performing and nonimproving elementary schools (out of the 4,000 total) receive resources and assistance to improve. And we do it without the schools' feeling stigmatized (another beneficial consequence of the six secrets in action).

Similarly, the secretariat has created a network of twenty-three school districts (five districts that are getting good new results and eighteen that are not moving forward) that work together for the improvement of all. All twenty-three district leaders voluntarily joined the network. In answer to those who object that organizations won't cooperate because of competition, we have found that time and again "bad" competition (you fail, I win) is replaced by "good" competition (how do we all get better, but I still want to improve as much as I can—friendly competition).

Have you ever seen Accenture's Tiger Woods ads? The ads show variations of his magnificent swing in diverse golf scenarios with different captions. There are fifteen of these ads at last count, and all of them relate to the themes in this book. Each ad is preceded by the phrase "We know what it takes to be a Tiger," and then shows a golf situation with a caption that labels a percentage breakdown on a 100 percent continuum. The tag line that best fits purposeful peer interaction across organizations is "Outperforms competitors: 49 percent. Outperforms self: 51 percent." With purposeful peer interaction, people band together to outperform themselves relative to their own past performance. We will discuss several more of these ads (and create one of our own) in subsequent chapters.

# The We-We Solution

*I*t is easy to miss the nuances of Secret Two. Peer interaction must be purposeful and must be characterized by high-capacity knowledge and skills (Secret Four). Leaders have to provide direction, create the conditions for effective peer interaction, and intervene along the way when things are not working as well as they could.

Three things are happening in the examples introduced in this chapter. First, all stakeholders are rallying around a *higher purpose* that has meaning for individuals as well as for the collectivity. As Taylor and LaBarre (2006) say about the maverick companies: "companies that are serious about understanding what makes their people tick equip their people with a serious understanding of what makes the company itself tick" (p. 243).

Second, *knowledge* flows as people pursue and continuously learn what works best. This feature will become especially clear when we take up Secret Three (capacity building prevails) and Four (learning is the work). These two components in effect furnish the content and substance, respectively, that make the crowd wiser. The continuous development and flow of knowledge is the intellectual lens that focuses the work on effective practices.

Third, *identifying* with an entity larger than oneself expands the self, with powerful consequences. Enlarged identity and commitment are the social glue that enable large organizations to cohere. We can take the building blocks in education as an example. When teachers within a school collaborate, they begin to think not just about "my classroom" but also about "our school." When school leaders work in a cluster of schools, they become almost as concerned about the success of other schools in the network as they do about their own. When district leaders participate in a network with other districts, they become interested in the success of other districts, and indeed the system as a whole.

The we-we commitment is fostered not because people fall in love with the hierarchy but because people fall in love with their peers (although if the hierarchy is pursuing a higher purpose and promoting peer learning, it becomes a beneficiary as well). In other words, the organization becomes effective because leaders are investing in employees, and this investment increases employees' individual and collective commitment to their work.

I am not naive. Companies and schools can certainly "win" in the short run by looking only after themselves. (This approach caused Peter Block, 1987, to ask, "why get better at a bad game?") And in certain cutthroat environments, it would be foolish to extend your hand to others. But the criteria for judging the validity of our traveling theory are these: Does the theory help explain actual situations of success? and, If used deliberately, will the theory result in similar successes in most cases? My answer is a resounding yes, as we saw in Sisodia et al.'s firms of endearment (discussed in Chapter One) and as we are experiencing time and again in our work in Ontario.

Peer interaction, as I have said, is not automatically good. Evolutionary theory tells us that the good side of peer interaction will have the upper hand and also tells us when to be careful (Sober & Wilson, 1998). In further work, Wilson (2007) studied what he calls "prosocial" orientation in teenagers. He incorporated seventeen items into a single index; one question, for example, was "For the job you expect to have in the future, how important is helping people?" The participants he calls "high-PRO" scored high on *social support, self-esteem,* and *planning for the future.* In terms of social support, high-PROs "have more teachers who care about them, neighbors who are more likely to help, and families more likely to avoid hurt feelings." On the self-esteem dimension, "the high-PROs are more hopeful for the future, energetically pursue their goals, and feel like a person of worth." And in terms of planning for the future, "high-PROs spend more time on homework after school, think more that it is important to have children and to provide them with opportunities, and expect to encounter obstacles (which they expect to overcome) compared to low-PROs"(p. 308). Overall, "high-PROs report that they are concentrating better; that they are living up to expectations of themselves and others; that they feel better about themselves; that they are happier, more active, social, involved and excited; that they are more challenged by activities that are more important and difficult; and that what they are doing is more interesting and relevant to their future goals" (p. 312).

Interestingly, although high-PROs are less likely to experience adverse events, when they did experience such events, "they were *more stressed* than low-PRO individuals" (p. 310; italics in original). An ounce of evolutionary thinking, says Wilson, tells you that no behavior is beneficial across all environments. Being high-PRO is hugely beneficial, "but only if you are in the bosom of a high-PRO social environment" (p. 312). This is one reason that firms of endearment generate so many benefits, including greater productivity. Wilson doesn't say this, but another ounce of evolutionary thinking will tell you that if it's a jungle out there—that is, if prosocial people find themselves in a negative environment—it won't take long for them to withdraw their services and themselves.

The implications of Wilson's research is that leaders should seek to create prosocial environments populated by prosocial individuals. Prosocials are not passive do-gooders. They do not simply go along with the crowd (only dead fish go with the flow, in the words of an interviewee quoted by Taylor & LaBarre, 2006). They are committed to getting important things done. Also none of the advice implied by the six secrets is meant to be taken literally; you probably want to take the dangers of groupthink into consideration, so a few dissenting mavericks are beneficial.

Further, you should stand for a high purpose, hire talented individuals along those lines, create mechanisms for purposeful peer interaction with a focus on results, and stay involved but avoid micromanaging. Put differently, once you establish the right conditions and set the process in motion, *trust the process and the people in it*. Don't choose between the hierarchy and the market—integrate them. Let the secrets do the work of monitoring: when peers interact with purpose, they provide their own built-in accountability, which does not require close monitoring but does benefit from the participation of the leader.

The theme of this chapter has been how to reconcile the too tight–too loose dilemma. The idea is to provide direction but be flexible along the way—or as another Accenture Tiger Woods ad illustrates: "flexible, 70 percent; unbending, 30 percent." The reason that you need purposeful peer interaction is that it is the group (led in the manner I describe in Chapters Three and Four) that can sort out consistency and flexibility—the tightness or looseness, as it were. Individuals working alone are sometimes better at solving simple problems, but well-functioning groups are always better at addressing challenging tasks, and there are few things as complex as making systems work their way to the future by integrating top-down, bottom-up, and lateral forces.

Working your way to the future requires combining the wisdom of the six secrets. Good theories travel when their constituent parts are cohesive. In this regard there is a close affinity between Secrets Two and Three.

‣SECRET ONE‣
## Love Your Employees

‣SECRET TWO‣
## Connect Peers with Purpose

SECRET THREE
## Capacity Building Prevails

‣SECRET FOUR‣
## Learning Is the Work

‣SECRET FIVE‣
## Transparency Rules

‣SECRET SIX‣
## Systems Learn

# SECRET · THREE

# Capacity Building Prevails

*A*nother way to love your employees is to select them well and then invest in their continuous development. In this chapter, I define capacity building, show how it is inversely related to judgmentalism, and indicate how to get started by selecting talented people. Chapter Four addresses what you do to operationalize capacity and keep developing it on the job. Bullying is not a good way to motivate people. When it comes to complex tasks, capacity building always trumps judgmentalism.

Capacity building concerns competencies, resources, and motivation. Individuals and groups are high in capacity if they possess and continue to develop knowledge and skills, if they attract and use resources (time, ideas, expertise, money) wisely, and if they are committed to putting in the energy to get important things done *collectively* and *continuously* (ever learning). This is a tall order in complex systems, but it is exactly the order required.

# Capacity Building Trumps Judgmentalism

One of the ways *not* to develop capacity is through criticism, punitive consequences, or what I more comprehensively call *judgmentalism*. Judgmentalism is not just seeing something as unacceptable or ineffective. It is that, but it is particularly harmful when it is accompanied by pejorative stigma, if you will excuse the redundancy. The advice here, especially for a new leader, is don't roll your eyes on day one when you see practice that is less than effective by your standards. Instead, invest in capacity building while suspending short-term judgment.

Canada's national newspaper, the *Globe and Mail,* ran an editorial on obesity titled "How Hectoring Backfires." The piece argued that intentions don't matter—if people feel stigmatized, they will not be motivated to change (2007). The consequences of insults or even good-natured advice aimed at overweight people are multiple and are all negative, including low self-esteem, vulnerability to depression, bad eating habits, avoidance of exercise, and general lethargy.

Hectoring is not motivating in any walk of life. People do not function well (at least not for very long) when they are scared and angry.

The difference between judgment and judgmentalism is brought out in a remarkable way in William Miller's book *Lincoln's Virtues* (2002). Lincoln did a good deal of concerted moral thinking about slavery, and his position was unequivocal: "if slavery is not wrong, nothing is wrong." This opinion may not sound remarkable today, but it was certainly not the norm in Indiana and Illinois, where Lincoln grew up and worked, let alone in the South. His moral stance on slavery is not the point here; it's how he used it to approach the problem. He avoided judgmentalism. Lincoln conceived his task as engaging in "joint efforts to accomplish *society-wide* goals through the instrument of government" (Miller, 2002, p. 105; italics added).

What was to become the mark of nonjudgmentalism in an older Lincoln was displayed in his early days when he was speaking to a group of ardent temperance advocates. Lincoln, himself a nondrinker, recommended the advice of "a sincere friend's sweet persuasion" rather than moral denunciation: "Assume to dictate to his judgment, or to command his action, or to mark him as one to be shunned and despised, and he will retreat within himself, close all the avenues to his head and his heart; and tho your cause be naked truth itself, transformed to the heaviest lance harder than steel can be made, and tho you throw it with more than Herculean force and precision, you shall no more be able to pierce him than to penetrate the hard shell of a tortoise with a rye straw" (quoted in Miller, 2002, pp. 148–149).

Lincoln knew that combining moral certitude with a hectoring change strategy would never work. Lincoln observed that those like himself and his listeners (steadfast nondrinkers) had never fallen victim to drink because they had "been spared more from absence of appetite than from any mental or moral superiority over those who have" (p. 150). Now that's nonjudgmentalism!

Nonjudgmentalism is a secret of change because it is so very heavily nuanced. You have to hold a strong moral position without succumbing to moral superiority as your sole change strategy. As Miller puts it, "When we strive for some great good or oppose some great evil, it is extremely difficult not to spill out some of the goodness onto ourselves and the evil onto our opponents, creating a deep *personal* moral gulf. It is very difficult, in other words, professing or striving for something righteous, to avoid self-righteousness and moral condemnation" (2002, p. 151; italics in original).

Lincoln's annual message to Congress in 1862 as president went to the heart of merging moral purpose and the goal of change. In talking about slavery he said, "we can succeed only in concert. It is not 'can *any* of us *imagine* better', but 'can we *all* do better'" (quoted in Miller, 2002, p. 224; italics in original). Unless you are literally going to kill all opposers, you had better have a more sophisticated change strategy.

In short, it is difficult in the extreme but still necessary to hold an unwavering moral position and to act explicitly from moral principles on given issues *while at the same time* not succumbing to the dead-end closure of judgmentalism.

In the day-to-day work of our organizations, we don't face issues as heavy as slavery. But what about failing to teach a seven-year-old living in poverty to read? Is that not a moral issue of great proportions when you extrapolate from that one child and realize the insidious consequences for both the individual and the society? In all situations of social change—what this book is all about—capacity building will trump judgmentalism. Judgment and capacity building *can* be combined. By contrast, moral certitude and raw fear are terrible change agents.

Pfeffer and Sutton (2000) identify five barriers to reducing what they call the "knowing-doing gap." One of these barriers is the fact that "fear prevents acting on knowledge." They found that organizations that were weak on generating and using knowledge had an atmosphere of fear and distrust.

In the intrinsically complex and uncertain world of today, problems get solved when people believe that they will not get punished for taking risks. In contrast, "when people fear for their jobs, their futures, or even for their self-esteem, it is unlikely that they will fear someone enough to do anything but what they have done in the past" (Pfeffer & Sutton, 2000, p. 110). Negative monitoring does not work. Risk taking based on knowledge and insight is essential to problem solving, and by definition will fail now and then. Of course, paying lip service instead of genuinely supporting risk taking is not sufficient. Samuel Goldwyn is reported to have said, "I want everyone to tell me the truth—even though it costs him his job."

Pfeffer and Sutton (2000) identify two other consequences of fear-induced change, both of which go against our secrets. The first is that fear causes a focus on the short term. Setting targets and providing financial rewards (whether in the stock market or in school achievement) by themselves are techniques in a theory of action that motivates people, all right—*motivates them to do the wrong things!* Manipulating figures, getting people to cut corners to achieve an all-important short-term goal, and downright fraud are some of the typical consequences.

Long-term thinking does not mean you ignore the short run. My colleagues and I are now able to say to political leaders, "Use certain ideas as the basis of your actions, and you can expect substantial positive results in student achievement within one election period (actually sooner)." Success can't be achieved overnight, but it is not open-ended either.

And Toyota's first (of fourteen) foundational management principles is "base your management decisions on a long-term philosophy, even at the expense of short-term financial goals" (Liker, 2004, p. 71). We are straight back to Secret One. Toyota's message is consistent and explicit: "*Do the right thing for the*

*company, its employees, the customer and society as a whole.*
Toyota's strong sense of mission and commitment to its customers,
employees and society is the *foundation for all the other principles*
and the missing ingredient in most companies trying to emulate
Toyota" (p. 72; italics in original). And like all firms of endearment, Toyota thrives and survives over long periods of time.

The second adverse consequence of fearmongering cited
by Pfeffer and Sutton (2000) is that it creates a focus on the
individual rather than the collective. Evolutionary theory once
more: when the environment turns nasty, people focus on self-
preservation. Managers become more concerned with taking credit
for their own good performance and blaming others for poor performance. One branch manager interviewed by Pfeffer and Sutton
"focused only on his individual performance throughout our
conversation, emphasizing the reasons he deserved more credit
than he was getting. He never once described anything that he
had done to help another branch manager, or described anything
that another manager had done to help him" (pp. 126–127).

Notice, too, that fear and its consequences directly contra-
vene Secret Two—the power and connectivity of positive peer
interaction. A trick question posed in another of Pfeffer's books
(2006): If you entered a hospital and had a choice of two wards,
would you choose Ward A or Ward B? Ward A has ten times the
number of reported errors as Ward B. But on closer inspection
it turns out that Ward B actually has more errors and, because it
operates in a climate of fear, covers them up and fails to acknowledge them. If you don't learn from failure, you fail to learn.
Forgive and remember, says Pfeffer.

Public education has a hard time learning these lessons.
With the punitive education policy of its No Child Left Behind

Act, the United States ranks far below the literacy and numeracy advancement of other countries. Using well-respected and validated measures of literacy and mathematics achievement for fifteen-year-olds, the Organization for Economic Cooperation and Development (OECD, which monitors the economic and social policies of the thirty-two richest nations in the world) found that the United States ranked twenty-second, compared to Finland, the Netherlands, and Canada, all of which rank in the top five and have nonpunitive assessment policies.

You don't make a pig fatter just by weighing it or by trying to scare it into eating. For organizational or systemic change, you actually have to motivate hordes of people to do something. As Pfeffer (2007) sarcastically says about urban education, describing it as America's hill to climb: "People have built quite successful careers—describing the hill, measuring the hill, walking around the hill, taking pictures of the hill, and so forth. Sooner or later, somebody needs to actually climb the hill" (p. 137).

Capacity building, not judgmentalism, is a hill-climbing secret. The formula is simple, but difficult to implement: start by taking the stigma out of the picture, and let pressure do its far more powerful work through the actions and interactions of the six secrets. The pressure that results from our secrets is more organically built into cultures. When peers interact purposefully, their expectations of one another create positive pressure to accomplish goals important to the group.

How do you work on capacity building? You start by attracting talented people and then you help them continually develop individually and collectively on the job (as I discuss in Chapter Four). Not as straightforward as it sounds.

# Hire and Cultivate Talented People

*T*oyota wins the prize for identifying (this chapter) and cultivating (next chapter) talent among all employees throughout the organization. I will go into more detail in the next
chapter because it is Toyota's ongoing learning culture that is
truly amazing. But the company starts by attracting good people
(because Toyota has a reputation for embodying the idea that
"good people working with other good people get even better").
People want to work there in the first place: "The truth is that
Toyota does like to start with good people who possess the *capacity* to become exceptional employees" (Liker & Meier, 2007, p. 18;
italics in original).

Toyota pays the same careful attention to selecting and developing managers and coaches. The attributes it looks for in trainers consist of willingness and ability to learn, adaptability and
flexibility, genuine caring and concern for others, patience, per-
sistence, willingness to take responsibility, confidence and leadership, and a questioning nature.

In the direct skill domain, Toyota stresses observation and
analytical ability, communication skills, attention to detail, job
knowledge, and respect of fellow employees (Liker & Meier,
2007, p. 72).

The successful maverick companies also reflect careful selection of talent that goes beyond credentials. In *Mavericks at Work*,
Taylor and LaBarre (2006) dig up a wonderful article from 1924
written by an anonymous business leader, titled "Why I Never
Hire Brilliant Men," in which the author states, "victory comes
to companies not through the employment of brilliant men,
but through knowing how to get the most out of *ordinary* folks"
(p. 199; italics in original). And Pfeffer (2007) warns us to be

careful with interviews: "the trouble is that showing up well in an interview is mostly based on looking good, sounding smart, and being verbally agile" (p. 89).

Remember that Enron's favorite brag was that it hired brilliant people. And remember the cage of the most productive hens, which murdered each other (Chapter Two). Taylor and LaBarre (2006) refer to Malcolm Gladwell's *New Yorker* essay "The Talent Myth," which asks, "What if smart people are overrated?" Individual stars do not make a sky; the system does.

Nothing I'm noting here is intended to eliminate intellectual prowess but to put it in perspective. Intelligence is overrated, as anyone who has read about emotional intelligence knows. The point is that intelligence must be linked with other qualities that are more difficult to learn and to discern. In *Mavericks at Work*, Taylor and LaBarre (2006), referring to Mike McCue of Tellme Network, put it well: "There's a difference between having great credentials and being a great contributor. McCue isn't just searching for the sharpest minds. He's probing for the closest fit. [According to McCue, people who thrive at Tellme] 'have a certain humility. They know they can get better; they want to learn from the best. We look for people who light up when they are around other talented people'" (p. 203).

They also quote another maverick leader who observes, "The best-performing companies I know don't just have a strong corporate culture, they have a deep-seated *recruiting* culture. They understand that recruiting is not some obscure function buried in the human resources bureaucracy. It is a prime driver of business success" (Taylor & LaBarre, 2006, p. 216). And Warner from Starbucks (one of the firms of endearment) states, "Our aim is to treat our candidates as well as we treat our customers" (p. 218). Secret One revisited.

In some ways, organizations that are on top of Secret Three turn the tables and constantly ask themselves (humbly and then confidently), "Why would great people want to work here?" And if they get that answer right, their employees become their best recruiters.

The most successful companies (as I define them through the six secrets) have decided that human resources is too important to leave to one unit. They have repositioned and refashioned human resources as a central, integrated prime driver of the corporate culture. This is true of all the firms of endearment. (Sisodia et al., 2007, wrote a whole chapter on "the decline and fall of human resources.") It is true of the maverick companies and of the ten "best managed" Canadian companies (one of which, Cirque du Soleil, is also on the maverick list). Another confirmatory resource is *Beyond HR: The New Science of Human Capital* (Boudreau & Ramstad, 2007), although I find this book a bit overly analytical and "techniquey."

The focus on attracting talent is equally important in the public sector, which does not have a great track record. Powerful confirmation of the difference the right talent can make in public schools comes from the McKinsey & Company report *How the World's Best-Performing School Systems Come out on Top* (Barber & Mourshed, 2007).

The McKinsey group visited and examined the top ten "high performers" on OECD's PISA 2003 assessment in literacy and mathematics: Australia, Belgium, Canada, England, Finland, Hong Kong, Japan, the Netherlands, New Zealand, and South Korea. McKinsey added Singapore, a non-PISA participant, because of high performance on other international comparisons. The group also analyzed fourteen other systems that were "strong improvers" (school districts, such as Boston, and countries, such as Bahrain and India). The findings focus on a compelling group of three interrelated sets of policies and practices.

McKinsey found that these systems (1) got more talented people to become teachers; (2) developed these teachers into better instructors, and for those becoming school principals, developed them into committed and talented school leaders; and (3) more effectively ensured that instructors consistently delivered the best possible instruction for every child in the system, including early and targeted intervention in the case of individual, school, or district underperformance. It is the first of these that concern us in this chapter.

Recall an earlier reference to the McKinsey report: "the quality of an education system cannot exceed the quality of its teachers" (Barber & Mourshed, 2007, p. 8). It continues, "The top performing school systems consistently attracted stronger people into the teaching profession, leading to better student outcomes. They did that by making entry into teaching training highly selective, developing effective processes for selecting the right applicants to becomes teachers, and paying good (but not great) starting compensation. Getting these essentials right drove up the status of the profession, which allowed it to attract even better candidates" (p. 8).

The very top performers recruited their teachers from the top one-third or higher of university graduates based on academic achievement (Finland, 10 percent; Singapore and Hong Kong, 30 percent; and South Korea, an astounding 5 percent). In Finland, all teachers—yes, 100 percent—are required to possess a master's degree. All of these countries avoided the pitfalls of recruitment based solely on academic grades. They assessed

## Exhibit 3.1: Singapore: Selection of Teachers

| | |
|---|---|
| **CV screen** | • *Check for minimum:*<br>– Academically, applicants should be in the top 30% of their age cohort<br>– Applicants should have completed relevant school and university education<br>– Applicants must show evidence of interest in children and education |
| **Assessment tests** | • *Check literacy:*<br>– Applicants must have a high level of literacy<br>– Evidence shows that teachers' literacy affects achievement more than any other measurable variable |
| **Interviews** | • *Check attitude, aptitude and personality:*<br>– Conducted by a panel of three experienced headmasters<br>– May include practical tests or activities |
| **Monitoring at NIE** | • *Check attitude, aptitude and personality:*<br>– Teachers are monitored during their initial teacher training at NIE<br>– A small number of candidates who do not demonstrate the required standards are removed from the course |

Only 1 in 6 applicants is accepted to become a teacher

*Source:* From *How the World's Best-Performing School Systems Come out on Top*, by M. Barber and M. Mourshed, 2007, London: McKinsey & Co. (Exhibit 7, on p. 17). Permission to reproduce exhibit granted by authors.

and screened for "a high overall level of literacy and numeracy, strong interpersonal and communication skills, willingness to learn, and motivation to teach" (p. 9), which included, lo and behold, the love of enabling children to learn.

Exhibits 3.1 and 3.2 illustrate Singapore's and Finland's teacher selection processes.

In some countries, the government set out to improve the status and attractiveness of the teaching profession through a combination of carefully constructed marketing strategies, backed up by better and more financially supported teaching training and

## Exhibit 3.2: Finland: Selection of Teachers

| | |
|---|---|
| **National screening** | • *Check for strong intrinsics:* 300-question multiple choice assessment testing numeracy, literacy and problem solving (from 2007; the first round was previously based on high school grades and other factors) |
| **Assessment tests (university)** | • *Check overall academic ability and literacy:*<br>– Tests evaluate the ability to process information, think critically, and synthesise data<br>– Applicants should be in the top 20% of their cohort |
| **Interviews (university)** | • *Check suitability for teaching:* Interviews look for motivation to teach, motivation to learn, communication skills and emotional intelligence |
| **Group work (university)** | • *Check suitability for teaching:* Group exercises and teaching demonstrations test communications and interpersonal skills |
| **Recruitment by school** | • On completion of their teacher training, candidates are recruited by individual schools |

Only 1 in 10 applicants is accepted to become a teacher*

*Source:* From *How the World's Best-Performing School Systems Come out on Top*, by M. Barber and M. Mourshed, 2007, London: McKinsey & Co. (Exhibit 9, on p. 17). Permission to reproduce exhibit granted by the authors.

better starting salaries. England, for example, made the teaching profession the most popular profession among undergraduates and graduates ages twenty-one to thirty-six in just five years.

Equally explicit attention was paid to the development of leaders, literacy coaches, and school principals. These systems took to heart the research finding of my colleague Ken Leithwood that "school leadership is second only to classroom teaching as an influence on learning" (Leithwood, Louis, Anderson, & Wahlstrom, 2004). However, in my own research I have found that principals have a difficult time focusing on intense instructional leadership

## Exhibit 3.3: Boston: Developing Principals

| Fellowship program | • 3 days a week on apprenticeship in schools, working with an experienced principal<br>• 2 days a week in classes and seminars, focused on management techniques, and instructional leadership<br>• Fellows are paid a salary during training; they compete for principal positions on graduation |
|---|---|
| New principal support | • *Summer institute:* A five-day program focused on preparing principals for their first 2–3 weeks in the school<br>• *Mentoring:* Each new principal is mentored by an experienced principal with a complementary set of skills<br>• *Central Support* on administrative issues, e.g. school budgeting<br>• *Networking meetings:* monthly facilitated cohort meetings<br>• *Just-in-time sessions:* Seminars or workshops for the cohort group to cover specific problem areas, as requested |
| On-going development | • *Deputy Superintendents:* Boston requires that deputy superintendents devote most of their time to coaching principals<br>• *Clusters:* The district is divided into 9 clusters, each with a cluster leader. The cluster leader provides mentoring and support for other principals in the cluster, without having a direct evaluative or supervisory role |

*Source:* From *How the World's Best-Performing School Systems Come out on Top*, by M. Barber and M. Mourshed, 2007, London: McKinsey & Co. (Exhibit 19, on p. 31). Permission to reproduce exhibit granted by the authors.

## Exhibit 3.4: Singapore: Beyond Best Practice

*"We train our teachers and vice-principals to apply best practices; we train our principals to create them"*

| Six month program to develop new principals | • **Management and leadership courses** taken from leading executive training programs<br>• **One day a week in schools** where candidates are assigned to develop innovative approaches to the toughest problems that the school faces<br>• **Group projects** where candidates work as teams to develop new educational approaches<br>• **2-week overseas placement** with a foreign corporation (e.g. IBM, HP, Ritz Carlton), where they shadow top private-sector executives in order to gain a private-sector perspective on distinctive leadership<br>• **Rigorous evaluation** – only candidates who demonstrate the required competencies will be appointed as a principal |
|---|---|

*Source:* From *How the World's Best-Performing School Systems Come out on Top*, by M. Barber and M. Mourshed, 2007, London: McKinsey & Co. (Exhibit 20, on p. 31). Permission to reproduce exhibit granted by the authors.

practices (Fullan, 2006). The system needs to enhance the role of the principal as instructional leader, as Boston and Singapore are doing, and as illustrated in Exhibits 3.3 and 3.4.

In all organizations, leaders have to go out of their way to recruit talented people who are fit for the purpose at hand—fit to work in organizations that thrive by embracing the six secrets. In other words, these organizations seek people who are not only individually talented but also *system* talented—that is, they can work in and keep developing cultures of purposeful collaboration. I endorse Pfeffer and Sutton's concern that "an obsession with individual 'talent' can be hazardous to organizational health" (2006, p. 90.) You are much better off hiring for purpose and hiring for *potential*—potential to learn on the job, both individually and with others. "Talent isn't fixed—unless you believe it is," say Pfeffer and Sutton (2006, p. 92). In fact, talent depends on people's motivation and experiences: "talent depends on how a person is managed or led" (p. 92).

We have seen in this chapter that the principle of choosing capacity building over judgmentalism applies in all types of systems, whether they focus on changing society or they operate in public and private organizations within society. Bullies try to take shortcuts to the detriment of all. Capacity building starts with hiring people who have potential. But—and this is a big but—once you get good people in the door, you had better offer them something good: How are you going to keep them down on the farm after they've seen the farm?

This takes us into Chapter Four, which explores how better farms operate.

·SECRET ONE·
Love Your Employees

·SECRET TWO·
Connect Peers with Purpose

·SECRET THREE·
Capacity Building Prevails

SECRET FOUR
**Learning Is the Work**

·SECRET FIVE·
Transparency Rules

·SECRET SIX·
Systems Learn

# Learning Is the Work

emember Frederick Taylor and his principles of scientific management, by which he taught a laborer how to lift tons of pig iron four times more efficiently? Taylor was on the right track, but his approach was too literal and too dehumanized. (Being an engineer, he approached the problem as a technical one.)

We need to get some terms straight before delving into Secret Four. Frederick Taylor sought *prescription*. Today we need to figure out and pursue *precision*. Taylor wanted to achieve 100 percent efficiency, whereas we need to strike a dynamic balance between *consistency* and *innovation*. Here's another Accenture Tiger Woods ad: "relentless consistency, 50 percent; willingness to change, 50 percent." Jobs vary in their degree of routine versus nonroutine work, but we will see in this chapter that the consistency-innovation continuum applies to all jobs, whether they involve doctors and nurses washing their hands, automobile manufacturing, the use of intravenous catheters, improving literacy, or reducing the number of high school dropouts.

The essence of Secret Four concerns how organizations address their core goals and tasks with relentless consistency, while at the same time learning continuously how to get better and better at what they are doing. In this chapter we will consider how to reconcile the consistency-innovation dilemma in a variety of settings. I will be precise by using concrete examples. And then we will see how organizations go about ensuring that consistency and innovation get built into the culture of everyday work.

The secret behind "learning is the work" lies in our integration of the precision needed for consistent performance (using what we already know) with the new learning required for continuous improvement. Once again, the "opposable mind" at work can resolve problems that appear to be mutually exclusive (Martin, 2007).

## What Consistency and Innovation Look Like

*A*tul Gawande (2007) is a general surgeon at the Brigham and Women's Hospital in Boston. His most recent book, *Better,* offers great concrete examples demonstrating how organizations need to diligently and consistently apply what they know, while seeking equally how to get better at what they do.

Let's start with a seemingly straightforward task: doctors and nurses regularly washing their hands. Gawande (2007) reports that every year, two million Americans acquire an infection while they are in a hospital and that ninety thousand die from that infection. Yet one of the greatest difficulties hospital administrators have "is getting clinicians like me to do the one thing that consistently halts the spread of infections: wash your hands" (p. 14). Hospital statistics show that "we doctors and nurses wash our hands one-third to one-half as often as we are supposed to" (p. 15). Precision also involves the pursuit of perfection. Even when compliance rates for proper hand hygiene were improved, increasing to 70 percent from 40 percent in Gawande's hospital, infection rates did not decline—because that 30 percent who did not wash their hands still left plenty of opportunities to continue transmitting infections.

As we will see with each of the examples in the chapter, successful organizations mobilize themselves to be *"all over"* the *practices that are known to make a difference.* In Gawande's hospital, anything short of an "obsession with hand washing has begun to seem inadequate" (2007, p. 20). It took consistent education, convenience of hand-washing facilities, and frequent random spot checks to monitor and improve performance on something as simple as washing one's hands regularly.

Going from the ridiculous to the sublime, Gawande talks of consistency and innovation in dealing with soldiers wounded in war. He describes visiting Walter Reed Army Medical Center in Washington D.C., where he observed case after case. "These were all terrible and formidable injuries. Nonetheless, all were saved" (2007, p. 54).

The key to this remarkable performance, says Gawande, was not attributable to new technologies or to any special skills of doctors. No, the answer involved none other than our theme here: the pursuit of consistency and innovations grounded in the work at hand. "To make a science of performance, to investigate and improve how well they use the knowledge and technologies they already have at hand, the doctors told me of simple, almost banal changes that produced enormous improvements" (2007, p. 56).

These improvements included getting soldiers to wear their Kevlar vests, and teaching medics how to administer to wounded soldiers in the first "golden hour" before transporting them.

Gawande says that making improvements under difficult circumstances tend to cultivate habits of "diligence," "doing it right," and "ingenuity." It is not waiting for the answer from research (although it does entail continuously seeking knowledge). As Gawande put it, "in the absence of certainty, the truth is that we want doctors who fight. . . . Always fight. Always look for what more you could do" (2007, p. 159). This spirit likewise pervades my book *What's Worth Fighting for in the Principalship* (Fullan, 2008).

In a refrain that resonates across the six secrets, Gawande quotes a leading medical reformer: "to fix medicine we need to do two things: measure ourselves and be open about what we are doing" (2007, p. 214).

We see time and again that new technology is usually not the best way to spur creative breakthroughs. Rather, "the infant science of improving performance," as Gawande calls it (2007, p. 242), proves more helpful. Gawande might as well have been writing about Toyota.

Toyota has made a science of improving performance. Liker and Meier (2007) give chapter and verse in their study of the culture of continuous improvement at Toyota. The essence of Toyota's approach to improved performance in all areas of work consists of three components: (1) identify critical knowledge; (2) transfer knowledge using job instruction; and (3) verify learning and success. As Liker and Meier observe, this is not a "project" but rather "a process [that] will require continued, sustained effort *forever*" (p. 82; italics in original).

Liker and Meier make the critical point that going about identifying and standardizing critical knowledge is not just for technical tasks, such as those performed on assembly lines, but applies to all jobs. To illustrate this they use three examples: manufacturing (bumper molder operator), a nurse in a busy hospital, and an entry-level design engineer. This universal applicability is a key message of Secret Four: consistency and innovation can and must go together, and you achieve them through organized learning in context. Learning *is* the work.

I won't go into the technical details of the three examples, but we do need to appreciate what is going on in these cases. Liker and Meier note, "We estimate that Toyota spends five times as much time detailing work methods and developing talent in employees as any other company we have seen" (2007, p. 110). Later they state, "If we were to identify the single greatest difference between Toyota and other organizations (this includes service, healthcare, and manufacturing organizations) it would be *the depth of understanding* among Toyota employees regarding their work" (p. 112; italics added).

On the question of whether focusing on the consistency of practice inhibits creativity, Liker and Meier provide the answer to whether Toyota is producing "mindless conformity or intentional mindfulness." Toyota placed a very high value on "creativity, thinking ability and problem-solving" (2007, p. 113). When the preoccupation is with the science of improving performance, you can be like Tiger Woods: nail down the common practices that work so that you can get consistent results; *at the same time,* you are freeing up energy for working on innovative practices that get even greater results.

The intent of standardized work is not to make all work highly repetitive, giving license to neo-Taylorites to robotosize every task. Rather, the intent is to define the best methods for reducing variation in favor of practices that are known to be effective, identifying the few key practices that are crucial to success. Not for 100 percent of the work, but for the aspects that are critical. In most cases, write Liker and Meier, "the critical aspects of any work equal about 15 to 20 percent of the total work" (2007, p. 143). The key is to identify those aspects and to take special care that everyone does those tasks well using the known best method of doing so. And "for these items there is no acceptable deviation from the defined method" (p. 144).

Liker and Meier (2007) then apply this approach to analyzing the tasks of the busy hospital nurse. After categorizing all aspects of the job into "core" and "ancillary" tasks, they further break them down into routine and nonroutine elements. For purposes of illustration, I will mention only one of these: starting an IV in a peripheral vein. Liker and Meier identify six main steps: (1) stabilize the vein; (2) place tip of needle against the skin; (3) depress skin with needle; (4) puncture skin with needle; (5) change needle angle; and (6) advance the catheter. For each of the six steps, the authors identify "key points" with respect to safety, quality, technique, and cost.

No part of the work of consistent effective performance is static. In the midst of any action, there is constant learning, whether it consists of detecting and correcting common errors or discovering new ways to improve. Later in this chapter, I will take up the question of *how* Toyota and other successful organizations do this, but for now I focus on what consistency and improvement look like in practice.

We can take up one final example from our work in improving literacy in schools and school districts. The parallels between our work and the work of firms like Toyota are eerie. In *Breakthrough,* Peter Hill, Carmel Crévola, and I argued for a more systematic approach to getting "breakthrough results" (virtually 100 percent of children becoming literate) and showed that we are partway there at present (Fullan, Hill, & Crévola, 2006). Building continuous improvement into the culture of the organization is the backbone of Secret Four.

The core concept of *Breakthrough* is the critical learning instructional path (CLIP), which is identical to Toyota's approach to "critical knowledge." The implementation of CLIP entails defining the route taken by the average learner in meeting a standard with respect to literacy performance. CLIP involves a set of steps to guide teachers and students toward the desired end points. The model incorporates monitoring where each student is at any point along the way and contains loops and detours so that instruction can be adjusted and focused on the learning needs of each and every child.

The following are the key messages in *Breakthrough:*

To make a substantial difference in outcomes, the next phase of reform must focus on what has typically been the "black box" in educational reform: classroom instruction.

The focus must be on improving classroom instruction and adopting processes that will create a more precise, validated, data-driven expert activity that can respond to the learning needs of individual students.

This focus requires diagnostic practitioners (teachers) who have a solid core of beliefs and understandings and a deep moral purpose, and who can develop highly personalized classroom programs.

A comprehensive focus requires systems that will support the day-to-day transformation of instruction for all students at all levels—systems that coordinate the literacy work of the classroom, the school, the district, and the state.

These systems will bring expert knowledge to bear on the detailed daily instructional decisions that teachers make. Maps of the pathways and detours followed by students in learning a defined area of the curriculum are constructed and built into CLIPs that serve as a framework for monitoring learning and guiding instruction.

As Toyota did, Hill, Crévola, and I developed CLIP on the workshop (classroom) floor. It was developed and refined working side by side with real teachers in real classrooms.

Also in a manner similar to Toyota, we describe CLIP as the pursuit of *precision,* not prescription. In collaboration with other teachers and instructional leaders, the teacher is constantly monitoring and making adjustments. The teacher has to be more, not less, creative than in traditional teaching—he or she is now engaged in intentional mindfulness, as Liker and Meier (2007) refer to it.

No school system has incorporated all elements of CLIP, and indeed that is the goal we advocate in *Breakthrough.* There are, however, many individual examples in action that incorporate many elements of CLIP and are getting results. I am going to describe, not the scores of elementary schools that are getting improved results in literacy, but rather an even more difficult example: high school reform.

Let's consider the problem of how to achieve 100 percent literacy for students. My colleagues and I have been working with York Region, just north of Toronto, for the past six years to improve literacy across all of its 181 schools (151 elementary and 30 high schools). Thornhill Secondary School in this region is a typical large high school with great ethnic diversity. Ontario has a mandatory grade 10 literacy test called the Ontario Secondary School Literacy Test (OSSLT). Students are required to pass this test to be eligible to graduate from high school. Students can take the test again if they fail on the first attempt.

Each June, as part of our systemwide strategy, York Region holds a "learning fair" in which all 181 schools display and convey what they have accomplished over the previous year. The following excerpts are from the Thornhill presentation in June 2007. Note that this presentation is prepared and presented entirely by the school—that is, these are the ideas and words of the school leaders themselves.

The school's plan of action includes a dual focus on building "teacher capacity for literacy instruction through shared leadership" coupled with an array of "student literacy programs and activities" led by teachers and by specially selected senior students as tutors. There is continuous, multifaceted data collection that is analyzed according to "successes and challenges." Successes are recognized; challenges are addressed. The whole approach is continuous and transparent to students, parents, teachers, and administrators alike.

When you get into the details of Thornhill's plan, you see relentless precision in action. For the 2006 literacy results, 88 percent of students taking the test were successful. The school knows, by name and profile, the forty-one students who did not pass (twenty-seven males, fourteen females; twenty-four ESL students; and so on). The school also knows the details about the students who were "previously eligible" and were taking the test for the second time or had had a deferral (for example, eleven of sixteen ESL students were unsuccessful).

Then we see the solutions at work. There are five overlapping interventions:

1. After-school literacy programs for ESL students

2. Workshops for small groups of students in grades 11 and 12 who have not yet passed the OSSLT

3. A "literacy blitz" for grade 10 students led by all teachers in the school, in all subjects, with additional time devoted to improving literacy in the weeks preceding the test

4. A hugely successful program called PLANT (Peer Literacy and Numeracy Team), in which selected students in grades 11 and 12 are trained and supported to work individually with struggling students who have not yet passed the OSSLT exam

5. A program called Guided Literacy Strategy, through which teachers provide individual tutoring

Every program is continually evaluated and refined. For example, the school conducts surveys that ask teachers and students how well the literacy blitz worked and how it should be improved. Every individual student who misses a session they should have attended is contacted by the literacy teachers or school administrator—not to be chastised, but to figure out how to increase participation. Students are surveyed to determine whether they are comfortable in attending sessions and are not made to feel stigmatized. The vast majority of students liked and appreciated the sessions.

Thornhill also compares its performance with the district's average as a whole (the thirty high schools) and the province's average, striving to better itself at each stage. Students are asked for details. Do you have a better understanding of each of the four segments of the OSSLT test: (1) multiple choice section on reading; (2) short writing tasks and newspaper article reviews; (3) interpreting brief passages and providing short answers; and (4) multiple choice and expression sections for writing? With respect to the PLANT program, to what extent has rapport been established between tutors and tutees? And so on.

There is nothing fancy about Thornhill's approach; it is just systematic and thorough, thanks to its application of Gawande's "science of improving performance." The school is so devoted to helping all its students become literate that it seems no student goes unnoticed. This level of attention is possible primarily because teachers sustain their willingness to improve with relentless consistency. But Thornhill is only one of 181 schools in the district. All schools in the system are learning from one other as they seek and implement effective literacy practices. Like Toyota, York Region works systematically as a district, building effectiveness into the operational culture of their system. They know that learning is the work.

So whether we're looking at implementing a hand-washing program, the treatment of casualties on the battlefield, automobile manufacturing, or improving literacy in schools, we see that all have Secret Four in common when they are successful.

This section set out to capture *what* consistency and innovation look like. Now the big question is, *How* do you put them in place? Given the details we have been discussing, you can probably guess that external workshops and courses won't do the trick.

In fact there is no trick: you can achieve consistency and innovation only through deep and consistent *learning in context.*

## Learn in Context or Learn Superficially

*L*earning on the job, day after day, is the work. My colleague Richard Elmore (2004) has nailed the problem of superficial learning in school reform. He notes that "improvement is more a function of learning to do the right thing in the setting in which you work" (p. 73). He elaborates: "The problem [is that] there is almost no opportunity for teachers to engage in continuous and substantial learning about their practice in the setting in which they actually work, observing and being observed by their colleagues in their own classrooms and classrooms of other teachers in other schools confronting similar problems of practice" (p. 127).

There is opportunity in Thornhill for teachers to learn in the setting in which they work. Learning is also built into our *Breakthrough* model where we combine personalization (identifying the learning needs of each and every individual), precision (responding accurately with the right focused instruction), and professional learning. Relative to the latter we concluded that breakthrough results were not possible unless *each and every teacher was learning how to improve every day.*

Instead, what we now have in most schools comes closer to professional development—what Peter Cole (2004) ruefully called "a great way to avoid change." Professional development programs or courses, even when they are good in themselves, are removed from the setting in which teachers work. At best they represent useful input, but only that. In contrast, when you combine the six secrets, you are building learning into the culture of the organization.

I have been talking about schools, but businesses do not fare any better on this dimension. Those that do, such as the companies named throughout this book, are successful precisely because they avoid superficial learning and instead embed philosophies and principles of learning in the specific contexts that need improvement. Nobody represents these values and practices better than Toyota. The company is exquisitely aware of Secret Four.

Toyota "gets" learning in context. Instead of workers leaving work to learn, learning is the job. Toyota's Job Instruction method is a top-notch training process because it is developed by using the job itself as the subject. The company selects and cultivates its leaders with one core purpose in mind: "Toyota's philosophy is every team leader and manager is a *teacher* first" (Liker & Meier, 2007, p. 283; italics added).

Thus, the most important job of any manager is to teach workers to become more effective: "the biggest success of any manager is the success of the people they have taught" (Liker & Meier, 2007, p. 313). For formal job instruction, on-the-job training is led by internal trainers and supervisors, who multiply their efforts by training others: "real learning comes from repeated practice with additional coaching from the trainer" (p. 246).

The success of the so-called student (the worker being trained) is the top priority. I cannot go into the details of training, but consider the following: "The student and the trainer would go to the workplace to observe the work being done by a skilled person. This will provide the student with an overall understanding of the work content and the necessary pace of the work. While observing, the trainer is able to explain the major steps and key points to the student" (Liker & Meier, 2007, p. 260).

When it comes to coaching and to student learning, the goal is to move the student toward self-reliance. Under the guidance of the supervisor, the "student performs the task while repeating the major steps" (p. 252), and the trainer "verifies understanding of the reasons for the key points" (p. 253), "corrects errors immediately to prevent bad habits" (p. 254), "assesses capability" (p. 255), and increasingly  "gives students responsibility" (p. 256), but keeps an eye on them (Liker & Meier, 2007). In Toyota's culture, as in all cultures where learning is the work, the trainer is always responsible for the student's success; if the student struggles, the trainer knows it is time to change the approach. Other principles include the following: always support the student, explain whom to call for help, check progress frequently, encourage questions, and gradually reduce coaching and follow-up. Learning on the job is explicit, purposeful, and ubiquitous in these cultures.

One element of the overall philosophy overlaps Secret Three (capacity building prevails): "The objective is not to identify *whom* to blame for a problem, it is to find out where the *system* failed" (Liker & Meier, 2007, p. 289; italics in original). Without this philosophy, as we have noted, people have a tendency to hide problems, and consequently no one learns.

Our *Firms of Endearment* companies also embrace and enact a culture of learning (Sisodia et al., 2007). The Container Store, for example, provides 235 hours of training to first-year employees and 160 hours every year thereafter, all with a view to creating a culture where people learn from experience.

When I started my career forty years ago, I cut my teeth on the study of implementation, and have been studying, and increasingly doing it, ever since. In writing this chapter, I realize why it holds my interest: it is because implementation is the study of learning (or failing to learn) in context. Having a learning culture and the capacity to operate effectively "is much more important to organizational success than having the right strategy" (Pfeffer & Sutton, 2006, p. 145). Even Frederick Taylor, who was strongly prescriptive in his approach, refused a request by the Harvard Business School in 1908 to teach a course on his famous principles of scientific management, on the grounds that the ideas "could only be learned on the shop floor" (cited in Mintzberg, 2004, p. 39). Apparently Taylor knew more about learning in context than the dean. Mintzberg's point is not that nothing of value can be taught at the university, but rather that in the practical professions—teaching, management, medicine, law—whatever is taught must be steeped in learning through reflective action.

At the end of the last chapter, I said that this concept is comparable to creating better farms. What is a better farm? It is one where the work is meaningful and workers connect their own values to the overall purpose of the company. Good farms help people get better and better at what they do and what they can accomplish day after day. All successful companies know this. In *Mavericks at Work,* Taylor and LaBarre (2006) conclude, "If you want great people to do their best work, the logic goes, then you've got to create the right working conditions the moment they walk through the door" (p. 261). And then you have to keep creating cultures of learning every day that they are on the job. If people are not learning in the specific context in which the work is being done, they are inevitably learning superficially. Deep learning that is embedded in the culture of the workplace is the essence of Secret Four.

Secrets One through Four have set the stage for Secret Five—transparency rules. This is one of the most difficult secrets to grasp, because it depends on the other secrets. For organizations to survive and thrive in the twenty-first century, their leaders need to embrace and master the nuances of transparency.

·SECRET ONE·
## Love Your Employees

·SECRET TWO·
## Connect Peers with Purpose

·SECRET THREE·
## Capacity Building Prevails

·SECRET FOUR·
## Learning Is the Work

SECRET FIVE
## Transparency Rules

·SECRET SIX·
## Systems Learn

# SECRET › FIVE

# Transparency Rules

*T*he emperor is wearing no clothes, and the people like it. Transparency concerns assessing, communicating, and acting on data pertaining to the what, how, and outcomes of change efforts. All successful organizations know what transparency is not, what it is, and how they can use it as an essential tool for improvement.

## What Transparency Is Not

*F*irst, transparency is *not* measuring and reporting on everything under the sun. It is not attempting to use the measurement tail to wag the performance dog. It is not, for example, the U.S. government's educational policy, No Child Left Behind, with its ubiquitous Adequate Yearly Progress measurements. Transparency is not causing teachers to become what my colleagues Dennis Shirley and Andy Hargreaves (2006) characterized as "data-driven to distraction." It is insufficient to have strictly a *results orientation;* you also have to learn the processes and practices to achieve those desired results.

Liker and Meier (2007) make a similar point about Toyota's culture: "It does no good to find weakness, point it out, and then use retribution as a threat or expect it to be resolved on its own. The leader wants to find any weakness and correct it so the total system becomes stronger" (p. 290).

Second, transparency is not about gathering reams of data or measuring things that are not amenable to action. Information overload breeds confusion and clutter, not clarity.

Everyone knows that measures can focus attention, and many utter that superficial bromide "What gets measured gets done" (not always true—it depends on how you go about it). We noted earlier that pressured, punishment-based measurement systems cause people to look only after themselves and go for short-term results at the expense of more important goals. Pfeffer and Sutton (2000) finger measurement regimes that are too complex (too many separate measures), too subjective, or that miss important elements of performance: "Measures and the measurement process, especially badly designed or unnecessarily complex measurement systems, are among the biggest barriers to turning knowledge into action" (p. 139).

Instead, Pfeffer and Sutton say, "Measurements should be guides helping to direct behavior but not so powerful that they substitute for the judgment and wisdom that is so necessary to acquire knowledge and turn it into action" (p. 153). By calling for measurements that focus on selected outcomes and specific actions, they highlight one of the best ways of putting Secret Five into practice.

## What Effective Transparency Is

As usual, the best way to get at the applied, nuanced meaning of each secret is to analyze named organizations that are engaged in its use. Here I take up four such examples, in government, medicine, education, and business.

Michael Barber (2007), our friend with the big public portfolio (see the Introduction), is a good case in point. His job in Tony Blair's Prime Minister's Delivery Unit (PMDU) was to oversee the implementation of Blair's priorities in the areas of health, education, crime, and transport. Barber knows a great deal about effective transparency because his assignment under an intense public microscope was to translate "airy aspirations into specific measurable commitments" (p. 50). He and his colleagues did this by focusing on a small number of ambitious goals in each area, frequently gathering specific data on performance, conducting discussions that challenged poor performance, and working on specific capacity building in relation to the key challenges. Some of the particular issues included street crime, refugee applications, volume crime (for example, burglary), drugs, hospital emergency, waiting times for getting into hospitals, primary school literacy and numeracy, rail performance, and road congestion.

Barber tweaks Secret Three (in favor of judgmentalism) more than I recommend, but where we do agree totally is that transparency of performance must be front and center. We agree that in many cases the mere presence of transparent data can provide a powerful incentive for improvement, although we both go beyond mere presence into additional transparency—basic actions that are more likely to balance pressure and support so as to motivate action. Also, relative to Chapter Four, Barber's measurement approach is geared to achieving greater *precision* in implementing specific, consistent practices that produce results. He is unyieldingly prescriptive when it comes to the gathering and use of transparent data: "You have to be prescriptive in demanding that all providers gather data, identify best practices, apply them, and are then held accountable for results" (2007, p. 280). Barber's theory of action covers two of the Tiger Woods Accenture ads: "stick-to-it-iveness, 90 percent; intuitiveness, 10 percent"; and the only ad that totals more than 100 percent: "focus, 110 percent."

Gawande (2007), the surgeon seeking how medicine can become "better," makes similar points when he marvels at what is being done to gather data (used in turn to improve performance) under horrific battle conditions in Iraq: "[We] know the statistics of what happened to the wounded ... only because the medical teams took the time, despite the chaos and their fatigue to fill out the logs describing the injuries and their outcomes.... Three senior physicians took charge of collecting the data: they input more than 75 difference pieces of information on every casualty—all so they could later analyze the patterns of what had happened to the soldiers and how effective the treatment had been" (pp. 63–64).

Another example of data transparency and use comes from my colleagues' and my work to improve literacy and numeracy across the four thousand elementary schools in the public education system in Ontario. When we started the reform in October 2003, there was no available database, even though the provincial testing agency assessed reading, writing, and mathematics performance annually for all students in grades 3 and 6.

As part of the overall strategy, we created a new database, which we called "Statistical Neighbors." All four thousand schools are in the system. They are organized into four bands—students and schools from the most disadvantaged communities, two bands in the middle, and a fourth comprising students in the least disadvantaged communities. Schools can be examined using other categories as well—size of school, percentage of ESL students, geographical setting (rural or urban), and so on.

We are now in a position to use the data, and here is where the nuance of Secret Five comes into play. Simply publishing the results can possibly do some good, but more likely than not would have negative side effects. Instead we operate under a set of ground rules:

1. We do not condone starting with what the government in England calls League Tables—displaying the results of every school from lowest to highest scores without regard to context. Instead we do the following:
   a. Help schools compare themselves with themselves—that is, look at what progress they are making compared to previous years
   b. Help schools compare themselves with their statistical neighbors, comparing apples with apples
   c. Help schools examine their results relative to an external or absolute standard, such as how other schools in the province are faring and how close they are to achieving 100 percent success in literacy and numeracy

2. We work with the seventy-two school districts and their four thousand schools to set annual "aspirational targets" based on their current starting point.

3. We focus on capacity building, helping districts identify and use effective instructional practices.

4. Although we take each year's results seriously, we are cautious about drawing conclusions about any particular school based on just one year's results. We prefer to examine three-year trends to determine if schools or districts are "stuck" or "moving" (improving or declining).

5. For schools and districts that are continuing to under-
perform, we intervene with a program called Ontario
Focused Intervention Partnership (OFIP), which provides targeted help designed to improve performance.
There are currently about 1,100 of the 4,000 schools in
this program. We are careful not to stigmatize schools in
OFIP (in keeping with Secret Three), because doing so
gets people sidetracked into issues of blame.

Overall, we think that this approach to data-informed development is effective. There is quite a lot of pressure built into the
process, but that pressure is based on constructive transparency.
When data are precise, presented in a nonjudgmental way, con-
sidered by peers, and used for improvement as well as for external accountability, they serve to balance pressure and support.
This approach seems to work. After five years of flatlined results
before beginning the program (1999–2003), the province's literacy and numeracy scores have climbed by some 10 percentage
points, with OFIP schools improving more than the average.

Business firms that are especially successful also recognize and
embrace transparency. The twenty-eight firms of endearment
(Sisodia et al., 2007) self-consciously used transparency. Echo-
ing Friedman's *The World Is Flat* (2005), Sisodia et al. observe that
information is increasingly available to the masses, which in turn
is forcing companies to operate with increasing transparency: "But
that is no problem for companies with nothing to hide, as FoEs
have discovered. Transparency helps customers, employees and
other stakeholders develop trust in the company. It has proven to
be effective as a motivating force among employees" (p. 57).

Later they note, "FoEs generally share more information
with their employees than is the case for non-FoE companies.

FoE management knows that information is empowering and that liberally sharing financial and production information with employees develops a strong bridge of trust between employee and management. Moreover it helps to spur productivity against which to measure their efforts" (p. 222).

Transparency involves being open about results and practices and is essentially an exercise in pursuing and nailing down problems that recur and identifying evidence-informed responses to them.

Finally, Toyota takes transparency and sharing to a new level through its eleventh principle (of fourteen): "Respect your extended network of partners and suppliers by challenging them and helping them to improve" (Liker, 2004, p. 199). As one automotive supplier put it, "Toyota is more hands-on and more driven to improve their systems and then showing how that improves you" (p. 199). As I mentioned in an earlier chapter, Toyota goes so far as to give tours of its company to its competitors (not as risky as it sounds, because Toyota knows that culture cannot be stolen). It may be farfetched to expect individual business firms to contribute to the entire sector, but this aspiration is decidedly appropriate for the public sector. Indeed, our strategies for reforming education in Ontario include facilitating and expecting successful schools and districts and less successful ones *to openly learn from each other.* Transparency extended.

## Why Transparency Rules

*B*y *transparency* I mean openness about results. I also mean openness about what practices are most strongly connected to successful outcomes. What is inside the black box of implementation? How can we help others learn about and understand the inner workings of implementation? What is most effective? How can we hold all accountable for adopting what works best? These questions are the substance or content of transparency.

The first reason that transparency rules—or, more specifically, the reason we must embrace the idea that transparency rules—is that it is going to do so whether we like it or not. The flat-world access to information and the appetite for transparent accountability on the part of the public and various stakeholders and shareholders simply can no longer be thwarted.

The second reason that I say transparency rules is that it is a *good thing* on balance; in fact, it is essential to success. Yes, we all know that data can be misused. The public reporting of student results on a school-by-school (or teacher-by-teacher) basis can lead to unfair or destructive actions. However, the alternative— to keep the information private or to refuse even to collect it—is neither acceptable nor useful.

We see the simple power of what I call "mere transparency" in the economist Paul Collier's fascinating and disturbing account (2007) of the state of the world's poorest countries, *The Bottom Billion*. The hero, as Collier calls him, is Emmanuel Tumulsiime-Mutebile, now governor of the Central Bank of Uganda and formerly the permanent secretary of the Ministry of Finance and Planning. As Collier tells the story, when the Ministry of Finance devised a survey to track public expenditure, it came up with the depressing result that only 20 percent of the money that the government released for primary schools, other than for teachers' salaries, actually reached the schools. What to do?

> Obviously, one way would have been to tighten the top down system of audit and scrutiny, but they had already tried that

and it evidently wasn't working. So Tumulsiime-Mutebile decided to try a completely different approach: scrutiny from the bottom up. Each time the Ministry of Finance released money it informed the local media and it also sent a poster to each school setting out what it should be getting. . . . Three years later he repeated the tracking survey. Now, instead of 20 percent getting through to schools, 90 percent was getting through . . . so scrutiny turned 20 percent into 90 percent. More effective than doubling aid and doubling it again [p. 150].

A seemingly simplistic solution for an apparently intractable problem, but nevertheless an illustration of the power of mere transparency.

To move beyond mere transparency, we have to work on the conditions under which transparency can be used simultaneously for both improvement and accountability. We know that people will cover up and not report problems if the culture punishes them. So one thing we need to work on is developing cultures in which it is normal to experience problems and solve them as they occur—exactly what the organizations we have been discussing do. In other words, effective cultures embrace transparency and the use of data as a core part of their work.

Earlier in this book, I criticized aspects of Jack Welch's leadership style at GE. However, one of his great contributions was to alter GE's culture from one of bureaucratic obtuseness to one that embraced transparency of practice or, as he called it, "candor" (Welch, 2005). This did open up the culture to new ideas, although I would say that if you combine transparency with Welch's vitality curve, in which the bottom 10 percent of management gets fired annually (thereby violating Secret One), you are asking for trouble. The six secrets travel best as a pack.

The third reason that transparency rules is that in all cases of successful change, transparent data are used as a tool for improvement. You can't achieve better results without establishing mechanisms for open data collection and use. The solutions to perplexing problems of improving large organizations on a continuous basis are too nuanced and too contingent on precision under dynamic conditions for them to be discovered by individuals working in isolation. Transparency and the use of data on performance and practice can serve as powerful tools for improvement.

The fourth reason that transparency rules is that the credibility and long-term survival of organizations are dependent on public confidence. Call this external accountability. My colleagues and I have found that as leaders (principals and teachers) get better at using transparent data, two powerful outcomes transpire. These leaders start to positively value data on how well they are doing—with regard to successes and problems alike. They look forward to receiving data and learn to seek data that help them and that show them and others what is being accomplished. The second outcome is that they become more literate in assessment. They are able to explain themselves better. They become more comfortable entering conversations and debates on the meaning of the data and are able to hold their own when it comes to the interpretation and misinterpretation of information.

In his fable *The Three Signs of a Miserable Job,* Lencioni (2007) offers three ideas for avoiding the first sign of a miserable job, which he labels "immeasurement": "(1) employees need to be able to gauge their progress and level of contribution for themselves; (2) they cannot be fulfilled in their work if their success depends on the opinions or whims of another person, no matter how benevolent that person may be; and (3) without a tangible means for assessing success or failure, motivation eventually deteriorates as people see themselves as unable to control their own fate" (p. 222).

Lencioni argues, as I have done in this book, that people need to be able to compare themselves with themselves over time to assess their progress in achieving important personal and organizational goals. They can't do this without clear transparency showing the causal relationship between practice and results, which enables them to make corrections as they go. No doubt you are dying to know the other two signs of misery at the workplace. One is anonymity (being treated as a nonentity, which represents a violation of Secret One), and the other is irrelevance (the work is seen as unimportant to the supervisor and peers, which violates Secrets Two and Four, connect peers with purpose and learning is the work).

Transparency rules, then, because it is both inevitable and essential. When it is used effectively, the positive power of transparency is enormous. One could even say that transparency is a much more effective way of instilling fear (if that is the issue) than are hierarchical, punitive edicts. Barber (2007), in the public sector in England, and Collier (2007), in the absolutely poorest countries, both show that transparency is vital to all serious reform efforts.

This is the time to remind you that the secrets work together to serve as checks and balances in bringing out the best in a given secret while suppressing its riskier aspects. Working backwards from what we understand about the secrets we've discussed so far, we can say that transparency rules when it is combined with deep learning in context. Transparency and learning in context flourish when capacity building trumps judgmentalism, when peer interaction fosters coherence, and when employees and customers are equally valued. We have, in other words, a tapestry of secrets that serve organizational leaders in their bid to survive and thrive in complex times.

When you know that transparency is both inevitable and desirable for successful organizations, it becomes far less threatening. The emperor has no clothes, and he doesn't look so bad after all.

Leaders can make good headway by mastering Secrets One through Five. But if they really want to leave a legacy for future leaders in the organization, they must tackle the perennial problems of sociology and politics—how can systems learn now while establishing conditions for continued learning tomorrow?

·SECRET ONE·
**Love Your Employees**

·SECRET TWO·
**Connect Peers with Purpose**

·SECRET THREE·
**Capacity Building Prevails**

·SECRET FOUR·
**Learning Is the Work**

·SECRET FIVE·
**Transparency Rules**

SECRET SIX
**Systems Learn**

# SECRET · SIX

# Systems Learn

W hen the first five secrets are all put into play, the system can and often does learn, but even in the best systems, continuous learning is not guaranteed. Our starting point is that most organizations do *not* learn, and those that do, do not sustain their learning. In a study of "long-living" businesses, De Gues (1997) found that most companies failed to reach their fortieth birthday.

A key reason why organizations do not sustain learning is that they focus on *individual* leaders. As individual leaders come and go, the company engages in episodic ups (if they are lucky) and downs. Khurana's study (2002) of 850 CEOs in the United States captures the problem, which is reflected in the title of his book: *Searching for a Corporate Savior: The Irrational Quest for Charismatic CEOs*. Perversely, the poorer the performance of the company, the more likely it is that the board of directors will make the fundamental mistake of hiring a high-profile CEO, virtually guaranteeing discontinuity: "When a company performs badly, institutional investors are likely to demand that the CEO resign and be replaced by someone who is from outside the firm. The external CEO search process that ensues is characterized by unusual secrecy: anxious attention to the expectations of outsiders …; a focus on an extremely small number of candidates, people who are already high-profile leaders; and an emphasis on the elusive, culturally biased qualities of leadership and charisma at the expense of concrete knowledge of a firm and its problems" (Khurana, 2002, p. xii).

Andy Hargreaves and Dean Fink (2006) found similar punctuated discontinuity in their study of school principal succession. Using a matrix framework that cross-connects two dimensions, *planned to unplanned* and *continuous to discontinuous,* they found a great deal of unplanned discontinuity—in effect, randomness. Even in cases where new leaders were brought in to "turn around" a poorly performing school—let's call this potentially positive planned discontinuity—the staying power of initial success was limited.

> Discontinuity that is reversing a bad situation needs to be pushed with steadfastness over a long period of time, until it becomes the new continuity. While planned discontinuity can yield rapid results, its leadership needs time to consolidate the new culture, to embed it in the hearts and minds of everyone. Repeatedly, planned discontinuity was effective in shaking up the schools in our study but not at making changes stick. . . . Leaders of planned discontinuity in schools were transferred to struggling schools elsewhere long before their existing work had been completed. The result was a constant cycle of change throughout schools in the system but little lasting improvement in any one of them [2006, p. 69].

The end result, say Hargreaves and Fink, is a "perpetual carousel" where schools "move up and down with depressing regularity" (2006, p. 71). Recall from Chapter One that both

San Diego and Memphis school districts replaced their leaders with new superintendents who promptly and publicly reversed the reform policies of their predecessors.

If we know how organizations do *not* learn—and we know most of them don't—then how do systems learn? Basically in two ways. First, they focus on developing many leaders working in concert, instead of relying on key individuals. Second, they are led by people who approach complexity with a combination of humility and faith that effectiveness can be maximized under the circumstances. These leaders combine humility and confidence by incorporating the spirit and competencies of Secrets One through Five. Secret Six is a kind of metasecret and adds to the previous secrets.

## Focus on Many Leaders

*T*oyota is one of the twenty-eight firms of endearment, and I have discussed it at length. Pfeffer and Sutton (2006) go so far as to conclude that Toyota's performance "shows no *leadership effects*" (p. 211; italics in original). This is an odd statement on the face of it, because Toyota's culture is laced with leaders—and that is the point: "The fact that Toyota can succeed over decades . . . and that the company shows no *leadership effects*—or changes from succession—speaks to building a robust set of interrelated management practices and philosophies that provide advantage above and beyond the ideas or inspirations of single individuals" (p. 211; italics in original).

So the first half of Secret Six is to lace the culture with a theory that will travel over time, in which leadership manifests itself at all levels of the organization. Peter Senge (1990) became famous for suggesting that systems thinking was the key to coping with an ever more complex future. Essentially he said that the number of interdependent factors that existed in the simpler world of the past could be comprehended by a single smart person. Now, he states, the world has become so complex that no one individual can grasp or predict what might happen, because the number of interdependent factors at work and their ramifications are impossible to predict.

Senge's remedy was to increase the capacity to think systemically, in terms of the system as a whole, which would not resolve the problem, but would increase the probability of getting some of it right. An aside: the subsequent practical work of systems thinking has failed to produce leaders who can in accordance with system thinking. After all, Senge recommended that we develop a body of knowledge and related tools in order "to make the full patterns clearer, and *to help us see how to change them effectively*" (p. 7; italics added). Perhaps the failure to do this is related to the emphasis on system *thinking* rather system *doing*. And possibly it is related to the sheer megacomplexity of the twenty-first-century world.

The first task of Secret Six is to enact the first five secrets. By so doing, organizational members will feel valued and be valued (Secret One), be engaged in purposeful peer interaction that generates knowledge and commitment (Secret Two), build their individual and collective capacity (Secret Three), learn every day on the job (Secret Four), and experience the value of transparency in practice linked to marking progress (Secret Five). The net effect is a critical mass of organizational colleagues who are indeed learners. Because their worlds have in fact become enlarged through wider engagement inside and outside the organization, they have a broader system perspective and are more likely to act with the larger context in mind.

Because many leaders are working together, they are constantly cultivating leaders within their ranks for the future. Younger leaders are being groomed for the future of the organization, and when leaders develop other leaders in this way the likelihood of continuity and good direction is greatly enhanced.

This is the first half of Secret Six, but it is not sufficient on its own. In the meantime the environment is becoming ever more complex and uncertain—full of surprises. So how does a system learn under these conditions? It is going to take some doing to unravel this secret, but essentially it means being humble and confident at the same time and having the conceptual ideas and practical tools to operate in complex, unpredictable environments. This is system thinking and system doing at their best.

## Navigating Complex Terrain

The second half of Secret Six is humility, because the world is uncertain and, no matter what you do, you cannot guarantee a successful future. Part A says you can increase the probability of success; part B says that your success cannot be guaranteed. Let's use our traveling theory to create a new ad for Accenture and Tiger Woods (free of charge). It's derived from evolutionary theory: challenge the environment, 70 percent; adapt to the environment, 30 percent. Carnoustie and Augusta are very different golf settings, so Tiger Woods blends his relentless consistency with an openness to changing his game to suit the circumstances.

With respect to contemporary complexity, we have already discussed Thomas Friedman's *The World Is Flat* (2005). A more sophisticated and scarier treatment of the topic is Thomas Homer-Dixon's *The Upside of Down: Catastrophe, Creativity and the Renewal of Civilization* (2006). Read this book, and you will find that the possible end of civilization is only too plausible.

Homer-Dixon (2006, p. 11) bases his analysis on five "tectonic stresses":

1. Population stress arising from differences in the population growth rates between rich and poor societies, and from the spiraling growth of megacities in poor countries

2. Energy stress—above all from the increasing scarcity of conventional oil

3. Environmental stress from worsening damage to our land, water, forests, and fisheries

4. Climate stress from changes in the makeup of our atmosphere

5. Economic stress resulting from instabilities in the global economic system and ever-widening income gaps between rich and poor people

He goes on to observe: "The stressors and multipliers are a lethal mixture that sharply boosts the risk of collapse of the political, social, and economic order—an outcome I call *synchronous failure*" (2006, p. 16; italics in original). In his view, this convergence of stressors could occur at any time and in unpredictable patterns. The trigger effect of any crisis—political instability, economic consequences of severe oil price increases, the growing gap between the rich and the poor, or climate change—could ramify to produce synchronous failure. Because the range of permutations is large, Homer-Dixon recommends "we shouldn't be surprised by surprise" (p. 17).

Homer-Dixon presents fact after fact, case after case where stresses could converge in a way that can "fray a society's social fabric, erode its community, urban and government institutions; and foster civil violence, including riots, insurgency, guerilla warfare, and even ethnic cleansing" (2006, p. 149).

The statistics on the economics of poverty are also hair raising—about 1.1 billion people, or one-fifth of the population of the world's poor countries, live on less than what $1 a day would buy in the United States. And over the past century, the gap between the average income in poor countries and the average income in rich countries has widened. In 1870, the average income of rich countries was nine times greater than that of poor countries; in 1990, it was forty-five times greater (Homer-Dixon, 2006, p. 187). These circumstances are "producing a stew of changes and stresses that's an almost perfect recipe for widespread and even violent resentment of the world's rich by the world's poor . . . [producing] large numbers of people who are chronically dissatisfied with their lot" (p. 204).

A perfect situation for a perfect catastrophe. In times of upheaval, "the best lack all conviction, while the worst are full of passionate intensity" (W. B. Yeats).

What has this got to do with systems learning? The answer will become more clear as this chapter progresses, but we will begin with two elements: (1) since we know that the world is becoming more dynamically interrelated, all leaders need to be aware of the global system's potential impact on their businesses and on others, and (2) leaders can learn to cope with uncertainty. In the meantime, we need to round out the complexity picture.

If you can stand one more depressing topic, or, more accurately, if you are interested in a reality check about what will affect *all* of our futures, read Paul Collier's insightful analysis (2007) of the people living in the fifty-eight worst-off countries in the world. Believe it or not, none of these countries are on Homer-Dixon's watch list of troublesome countries in other words, they are worse off than the worst. They are small countries, but their combined populations total one billion of the world's six billion people. Most of these countries are in Africa and central Asia.

Whereas all other countries in the world, including some very poor countries, experienced unprecedented economic growth over the past forty years, people in the bottom-billion countries are actually poorer than they were in 1970. Collier shows how these countries are caught in one or more (usually more) of four deadly traps: the conflict trap, the natural resources trap (natural resources can actually be a detriment to longer-term growth), the trap of being landlocked with bad neighbors, and the trap of bad governance. Collier analyzes why aid by itself is not the answer. Rather he calls for a combination and careful sequencing of certain types of aid, selective military intervention (as in Rwanda and Darfur, not Iraq), laws and charters (including a charter for budget transparency), and targeted trade policies for reversing marginalization. This is not the place to delve into the details of the proposed solutions, but Collier warns that we ignore the plight of the bottom billion at our own peril (or, more accurately, at the future peril of our children and grandchildren): "I have a little boy of six. I do not want him to grow up in a world with a vast running sore—a billion people stuck in desperate conditions alongside unprecedented prosperity" (2007, p. 176).

When an economist starts worrying about moral purpose and the safety of his children, you know you have a problem.

Leaders at all levels in all companies in all countries—leaders who want to help others survive and thrive—need to be aware of the world's larger systemic problems. Leaders who have an affinity for the six secrets are more likely to realize that system learning does in fact mean the *entire* system—the global system. The awareness of the toxic global stew that Homer-Dixon and Collier so powerfully and relentlessly document helps explain why Toyota and the other twenty-seven firms of endearment are not satisfied to toil away in their little corner of the world. They have somehow realized that their stakeholders are not just investors and managers, but also employees and society—global society included. This larger context is extremely complex, and critical to all our futures. This kind of awareness is system learning writ large because it takes leaders, thinking well beyond their own organizations, and it does so in a relevant way. Leaders do need to know about their broader environments, for business reasons as well as altruistic ones. (See Ghemawat's 2007 detailed analysis of what leaders need to know and how they should approach global marketplaces.)

As leaders explore environmental complexity, they need to combine humility and confidence. Rosenzweig (2007) draws such a conclusion about respecting uncertainty. As we saw earlier, he warns us about the folly of deriving superficial lessons from apparently great companies after the fact—the so-called halo effect. He also tells us that no matter how prepared you are for the future, there are bound to be some uncertainties that you will not be able to control. Uncertain customer demand, unpredictable competitors, changing technology, and the uncertainties of execution (not to mention Homer-Dixon's tectonic stresses and Collier's bottom billion) unite to make the future a matter of good preparation and luck.

In Rosenzweig's (2007) view, managers who see the world without delusions are on the right track: "they are thoughtful leaders who recognize that success comes about from a combination of shrewd judgment and hard work with a dose of good luck mixed in, and they're well aware that if the breaks of the game had gone just a bit differently, the results could have been vastly different" (p.159).

In his book *In an Uncertain World,* Robert Rubin (2003), who was President Clinton's secretary of the treasury from 1995 to 1999, captures elements of Secret Six: "Some people I've encountered in various phases of my career seem more certain about everything than I am about anything. That kind of certainty . . . [represents] an attitude that seems to misunderstand the very nature of reality—its complexity and ambiguity—and thereby to provide a rather poor basis for working through decisions in a way that is likely to lead to better results" (p. xii).

What is needed instead, says Rubin, is for leaders to accept the concept of probabilistic decision making, and to consider the complexity of different factors that are likely to act and interact. This is an analytic process that also involves subjective judgment: "the ultimate decision then reflects all of this input but also instinct, experience and 'feel' (2003, p. xi). Risk taking by definition is not about getting results every time but about being successful in more situations than not. Rubin states it this way: "Even the best decisions about intervention are probabilistic and run the risk of failure, but failure wouldn't necessarily make the decision wrong" (p. 37).

Rosenzweig (2007) refers to this attitude as respect for complexity, "coupling humility in good times with an insistence on learning from bad times" (p.162). Or, as the Accenture Tiger Woods ad says, "playing it safe, 80 percent; knowing when not to, 20 percent." And, in his most recent ad, "plan, 70 percent; backup plan, 30 percent."

What these authors are saying is that no matter how smart you are, no matter how much you crunch the data, you can never be certain of a positive outcome. You can maximize your probability of success, but you can never be sure because of endemic complexity.

One thing we do know for sure. Leaders who operate from a position of certitude are bound to miss something, are likely to be wrong more than their share of times, and almost certainly will not learn from their experiences.

There is a paradox in Secret Six. On the one hand, followers expect leaders to know what they are doing, especially in relation to complex, critical issues of the day. On the other hand, leaders shouldn't be too sure of themselves. Paradoxes are to be finessed. Leaders need to convey confidence about the future even though they are not (should not be) fully certain. Stated differently, they can be confident that they have taken in to account all possibilities and have made the right choice under the circumstances, even though something may go wrong.

Rosabeth Moss Kanter (2004) puts it this way: "The fundamental task of leaders is to develop confidence in advance of victory in order to attract the investments that make victory possible—money, talent, support, empathy, attention, effort, or people's best thinking" (p. 19). In short, the advice to leaders is to set up processes that keep overconfidence in check. (Roberto, 2005, in *Why Great Leaders Don't Take Yes for an Answer,* has many strategies for so doing.) The advice to followers is not to put blind faith in leaders. Peter Drucker is reported to have said, "People refer to gurus because they don't know how to spell charlatan." So double-check all round.

Pfeffer and Sutton (2006), as they take us through the minefields of "hard facts, dangerous half-truths and total nonsense," end up with the most cogent advice. Their four paradoxes and corresponding guidelines (p. 200) are entirely compatible with Secret Six:

1. Everyone expects leaders to matter a lot, even as they have limited actual impact. Leaders need to act as if they are in control, project confidence, and talk about the future, even while recognizing and acknowledging the organizational realities and their own limitations.

2. Because leaders succumb to the same self-enhancement as everyone else, magnified by the adulation they receive, they have a tendency to lose their behavioral inhibitions and behave in destructive ways. They need to avoid this trap and maintain an attitude of wisdom and a healthy dose of modesty.

3. Because the desirability of exercising total control is itself a half-truth, effective leaders must learn when and how to get out of the way, and let others make contributions.

4. Leaders often have the most positive impact when they help build systems where a few powerful and magnificently skilled people matter the least. Perhaps the best way to view leadership is as a task of architecting organizational systems, teams, and cultures—as establishing the conditions and preconditions for others to succeed.

Out of these four paradoxes come four guidelines for action (Pfeffer & Sutton, 2006, p. 206):

1. Act and talk as if you were in control and project confidence.

2. Take credit and some blame.

3. Talk about the future.

4. Be specific about the few things that matter and keep repeating them.

These guidelines show the way toward mastery of Secret Six. Leaders need to be more confident in the face of complexity than the circumstances warrant, but not so certain that they ignore realities that don't fit their action plan. Secret Six entails grappling with system complexities, taking action, and then learning from the experiences—all while engaging other leaders, to increase chances that the organization as a whole will learn now and keep on learning.

In this framework, learning becomes more dynamic as leaders attempting to reconcile dilemmas at the system level. This type of system learning is most evident in Roger Martin's (2007) *The Opposable Mind*. After interviewing a variety of especially effective leaders from a broad range of contexts, Martin isolated one trait that all these leaders had in common. Because they could hold two diametrically opposing ideas in their heads without panicking or settling for one or the other idea, they were then able to "produce a synthesis that is superior to either opposing idea" (p. 6). He calls this capacity "integrative thinking" and defines it as "the ability to face constructively the tension of opposing ideas and, instead of choosing one at the expense of the other, generate a creative resolution of the tension in the form of a new idea that contains elements of the opposing ideas but is superior to each" (p. 15).

I trust it is not lost on readers that most of the secrets rely on just this sort of integrative thinking: for example, loving your employees and your customers (Secret One) and blending elements of both top-down and bottom-up thinking (Secret Two)—or, put another way, thinking in both-and terms rather than either-or terms. Martin's work is especially good at showing how leaders can acquire and enhance integrative thinking while de-emphasizing conventional thinking.

Integrative thinkers take a broader view of salient issues, try to figure out complex causality, visualize the whole while working on individual parts (what Martin calls the architecture of the problem), and eventually arrive at a creative resolution of tensions. Salience, causality, and architecture resolution are thus the elements of integrative problem solving (and, taken together, present a fair depiction of systems thinking).

Martin shows how to cultivate integrative thinking through constant iterations of stance, tools, and experiences, as follows:

*Stance.* Who am I in the world, and what am I trying to accomplish?

*Tools.* With what tools and models do I organize my thinking?

*Experiences.* With what experiences can I build my repertoire of sensitivities and skills [p. 103]?

Integrative thinkers, or Secret Six thinkers, do not accept existing models for defining reality, don't panic when addressing complexity (and instead look for patterns and causal relationships), are confident that a better, blended solution can be found, and view experiences as learning opportunities for developing both mastery and originality. In other words, they combine precision with creativity, as we saw in Secret Four (learning is the work) and its pairs of seemingly opposed illustrations of what it takes to be a tiger.

As Martin reminds us, tools must be constantly mediated though reflective stances and learning derived from new experiences. Everything I have said about Secrets One through Six is entirely consistent in form and content with his notion of the opposable mind. Although the secrets do require holding and reconciling opposing ideas, this complexity need not be overwhelming. The secrets, with practice and reflection, are accessible. By empowering you to lead with more confidence than the situation objectively warrants, the secrets make organizational life more vibrant and productive. Your track record over time becomes your credential. Complexity becomes less mysterious and more manageable.

If you stay the course on key moral principles, help develop leadership in others while being empathic about the challenges they are facing, and engage the wider environment in its complexity and uncertainty, you will ultimately discover how we can *all* do better. Pursue the first five secrets in concert, then add opposable learning to the mix. That's system learning.

# CONCLUSION
## *Keeping the Secrets*

SIX SECRETS ARE A LOT TO KEEP. BUT THESE ARE COMPLEX, dangerous times, so the secrets are all the more critical to internalize. Fortunately, there are some clear guidelines for doing so, which I will discuss here, and you will not be going it alone. Leaders from all quarters of the organization and the system at large must work on them together. These guidelines are for all types of leaders—branch plant managers, politicians, CEOs, community leaders—in both the public and private sectors. They are the guidelines necessary for leaders if they are to survive and thrive in the twenty-first century.

### Guidelines for Keeping the Secrets

1. Seize the synergy.

2. Define your own traveling theory.

3. Share a secret, keep a secret.

4. The world is the only oyster you have.

5. Stay on the far side of complexity.

6. Happiness is not what some of us think.

# Seize the Synergy

*F*ortunately, the secrets are so intertwined that working on any one means working on several simultaneously. To illustrate, let's look at just one iteration. As you love your employees as well as your customers (and other stakeholders) à la Secret One, you can focus on facilitating purposeful peer interaction (Secret Two), which endears employees to each other, the company, and customers. When you add capacity building sans judgmentalism, people grow without resentment (Secret Three). Throw in Secret Four, learning is the work, and people individually and collectively get much better at what they do, which further consolidates the first four secrets.

By employing the six secrets, we already have a fair amount of accountability built into the culture of the organization. Add ubiquitous transparency, and things firm up naturally because of the interplay among the secrets. For example, when you combine purposeful peer interaction, learning is the work, and transparency, strong internal accountability becomes inherently embedded in the culture. Take the stance that systems learn (Secret Six)—which means that you appreciate uncertainty and learn to get better at figuring out complexity and taking action, even when you know that not everything will necessarily turn out well—and you keep going. By doing all of this, you expand your perspective to incorporate both local and global contexts. All in all, you meet Pfeffer and Sutton's criterion for wisdom: "the ability to act with knowledge, while doubting what you know" (2006, p. 174).

# Define Your Own Traveling Theory

I have also argued from the Introduction onward that leaders need to develop and continually refine a good theory, defined as one that travels well in all kinds of situations. If you look for silver bullets and techniques, there is too much to remember, and you will not understand them deeply enough to use them all. I have offered a pretty good traveling theory in the six secrets.

Recall Wilson's definition of theory that we started with: "a theory is merely a way of organizing ideas that seem to make sense of the world" (2007, p. 16).

As I've noted elsewhere, a good theory explains not how you *want* the world to work, but how it *actually* works. Paradoxically, if you have strong moral principles along with a theory of change (as distinct from just having the moral principles), you have a greater chance of improving your organization and its environment. I recommend, then, that you work on your own theory. Obviously I think that the six secrets are on the mark because they stand up well when you apply them to a variety of situations, as I have done in this book. Use the six secrets to cause you to rethink or establish your own theory—one that is based on the secrets (I hope), but worked out so that the secrets make sense of what you are facing and what you want to accomplish.

Good theories are succinct. Action-based ideas are best expressed in five pages, rather than in fifty. When you know what you are doing, you can describe it accurately in fewer words. Oddly enough, though, when you don't know what you are doing, it takes longer to explain yourself! You really have to know what you are talking about to express it clearly and meaningfully.

## Share a Secret, Keep a Secret

*A*nother paradox: the best way to keep the secrets is to share them. If you practice the secrets, you model them for others. If you use them, you are at the same time developing other leaders who learn to know them. Implementing the six secrets and developing other leaders become one and the same. Once you have a culture of leaders at all levels operating in this way, they reinforce each other as they go.

This reinforcement produces, as mentioned in Chapter Six, the kind of culture that spurred Pfeffer and Sutton (2006) to draw the remarkable conclusion that over the years there had been no leadership effects at Toyota. In other words, no individual leader is indispensable, but leaders from all corners of the organization continue to move the organization forward because the *culture*—actions embedded in the norms, competencies, and practices of the organization—ensures it.

I hope it is clear also that you cannot teach the six secrets by micromanaging them—this is true by definition. It is very hard to avoid overmanaging when you know a lot as a leader. The more you know, the more you want to control. But this is precisely the point: leaders who thrive and survive are people who know they don't know everything. In fact this knowledge—knowing that you don't know—is crucial for enabling others. Pfeffer and Sutton (2006) convey the need to let go in the following words: "The mindset . . . entails . . . being willing to let go and let other people perform, develop, learn, and make mistakes. It is hard to build a system where others can succeed if the leader believes he or she needs to make every important decision, and knows better than anyone else what to do and how to do it. It is in finding the balance between guidance and listening, between directing and learning, that those in leadership roles can make their most useful contributions to organization performance" (p. 211).

We have built our education reform strategy in Ontario on this combination of direction and confidence building from the center, and flexibility in allowing and seeking leadership at all levels of the system. If you lace the system with purposeful vertical and horizontal interaction along with transparency of data, you can trust the system to perform well more times than not—and more than any other approach. By putting the secrets in action, you inspire effective actions from others.

## The World Is the Only Oyster You Have

"The world is your oyster" has traditionally meant the world is yours for the taking. We have seen that this is not the case under conditions of growing complexity. The secrets, however, do increase your chances of success by engaging the larger world on your terms. The world is not for your taking, but it is for your *making*. Time and again we have seen the scope of leadership enlarged. We saw it in Sisodia et al.'s comprehensive definition (2007) of stakeholders: employees, customers, investors, partners, and society. The needs of *all five* must be addressed and treated in a balanced way: "Each of these relationships must be managed in a way that (a) a two-way flow of value exists between both parties to the relationship and (b) the interests of both parties are aligned" (p. 54).

The potential benefits from this approach are unlimited. When people learn from each other, everyone can gain without taking away from others. This is one case where the whole is truly greater than the sum of its parts. The goal is to embrace and contribute to many levels of the system simultaneously.

Mintzberg (2004) draws a similar conclusion: "I believe the role of . . . management is . . . to promote organization development to attain social development. In other words, *how* we serve our purpose is by developing better managers to improve organizations. *Why* we do this is to create a better society" (p. 379; italics in original).

Any narrower definition of who is the stakeholder glorifies selfishness to the detriment of all.

The satisfaction and necessity of teaching other leaders to survive and thrive is another component of treating the world beyond yourself as the only oyster you have. Help improve it or suffer the consequences locally.

As Mintzberg puts it: "Leadership is not about making clever decisions and doing bigger deals, least of all for personal gain. It is about energizing other people to make good decisions and do other things. In other words, it is about helping release the positive energy that exists naturally within people. Effective leadership inspires more than empowers; it connects more than controls; it demonstrates more than it decides. It does all of this by *engaging*— itself above all and consequently others" (2004, p. 143).

In a similar vein, Pfeffer and Sutton (2006) recommend that leaders create an atmosphere where people constantly learn from each other as they face internal and external realities. Treating others as leaders in the making is the best way to attract and retain great people who will in turn make the organization great.

The big oyster is the world at large, the one that Homer-Dixon (2006) and Collier (2007) told us about in Chapter Six. If the world as a whole is not on your worry list, it should be. To reach the core of human and societal values, we must acknowledge our place in the larger environment. And paradoxical as it may seem, when we contribute to the betterment of the environments in which we work, we are also serving our self-interest. Identifying specific values sometimes becomes controversial, so I've found Homer-Dixon's delineation of three broad categories of values very useful. He says there are *utilitarian* values, which are "simple likes and dislikes"; *moral* values, which "concern fairness and justice, especially regarding things like the distribution of wealth, power, and opportunity among people"; and *existential* values, which "apply to things that give our lives significance and meaning" (p. 301; italics in original).

Our values, according to Homer-Dixon (2006), are out of whack:

> Because we're reluctant or unable to talk about moral and existential values—and these values remain largely unexplored—utilitarian values fill the void. This is one reason why consumerism has developed such a firm grip on the psyches of so many of us in the West. Without a coherent notion of what gives our lives meaning we try to satisfy our need for meaning by buying more stuff. . . . Reduced to walking appetites we lose resilience. We risk becoming hollow people with no character, substance and core—like eggshells that can be shattered or crushed with some sharp shock [p. 302].

Acting with integrity and assisting those with whom you work in plugging into a wider, more meaningful idea of how and where your company fits with society are essential for the survival of your organization because context is everything. Context can expand or constrain our opportunities to grow, so we have a vested interest in helping improve it. If moral values sound too religious or too left wing, existential values will do. They concern improving the lot of those around us through leadership that maximizes the beneficial impact of the six secrets at work. This is as moral as humans need to get.

## Stay on the Far Side of Complexity

Working on the near side of complexity means seeking silver bullets. It means being "techniquey"—seeking tools as solutions instead of getting at the underlying issues. Staying on the far side entails recognizing complexity without succumbing to it. Sisodia et al. (2007) quote Oliver Wendell Holmes: "I would not give a fig for the simplicity this side of complexity but I would give my life for the simplicity on the other side of complexity" (p. 256). They then quote James O'Toole (1995): "To move beyond the confusion of complexity, executives must abandon their constant search for the immediately practical and, paradoxically, seek to understand the underlying ideas and values that have shaped the world they work in. Managers who clamor for how-to instruction are, by definition, stuck on the near side of complexity" (quoted in Sisodia et al., 2007, p. 256).

Because the secrets are so grounded in action, working on the far side of complexity is not an abstract exercise. It requires, as we have seen, balancing confidence and humility while also reconciling complexity. Taylor and LaBarre (2006) call this stance a blend of "personal confidence and intellectual humility" (p. 110).

In using the secrets, leaders in effect reduce large chunks of uncertainty because they get at better and more complete evidence and understanding. Once they have stripped away all the uncertainty that is possible to discern, they are in a better position to deal with the remaining complexity—that is, the complexity that is impossible to comprehend in advance. Complexity may defeat you in some circumstances, but it will *always* defeat you if you ignore it. Staying on the far side of complexity—essentially what I advocated in Secret Six—is a full-time job.

## Happiness Is Not What Some of Us Think

*T*he sheer wealth of a society does not make people happier, even if they are among the rich. (For the very poor, however, lack of basic necessities means lives of misery and degradation, especially where the gap between the rich and the poor is wide.) The health economist Richard Wilkinson (2005) reveals the many negative consequences of such inequality in societies. Beyond a certain level of wealth, getting richer is at best neutral. Wilkinson quotes Frank (1999): "Study after careful study shows that beyond some point, the average happiness within a country is completely unaffected by increases in its average income level" (p. 111).

The trouble is that unchecked capitalism and its associated utilitarian values are hard to curb once they are in place—more wants more. The sheer growth imperative, as Homer-Dixon calls it, eventually overloads society to the point of breakdown. Breakdown will occur, he warns, even if people are playing by the rules. This means we have go beyond the rules and explicitly reduce consumption. Collier (2007) identifies the added problem that people in power under loose conditions have a tendency to help themselves.

We can also see the negative effects when organizations define success only in terms of growth and accomplishment of targets at all cost. This is Sheth's self-destructive habit (2007) number six: volume obsession—growth for the sake of growth.

To see the real-life results of leaders' use (or violation) of the Six Secrets, consider the leadership styles of two great Antarctic explorers. Both Robert F. Scott and Sir Ernest Shackleton were incredibly determined to lead their crews to the South Pole in the early 1900s, but the results of the two expeditions were dramatically different. Shackleton combined meaningful challenge with a concern for his followers, but for Scott finishing was the only goal that counted. Happiness requires combining meaningful work with regard for others.

Morrell and Capparell (2001) contrast the elements of Shackleton's style with Scott's thusly: "Scott . . . was rigid and formal. For him the prize was paramount and his military training would have dictated that some loss of life was inevitable. . . . Scott was dour, bullying and controlling; Shackleton was warm, humorous and egalitarian. . . . Scott tried to orchestrate every movement of his men; Shackleton gave his men responsibility and some measure of independence. Scott was secretive and untrusting; Shackleton talked openly and frankly with the men about all aspects of the work. Scott put his team at risk to achieve his goals; Shackleton valued his men's lives above all else" (p. 36).

Scott's men died. All of Shackleton's men survived the wreck of their ship, *Endurance,* in the crushing Antarctic ice, stranded twelve thousand miles from civilization with no means of communication. Isolated for almost two years on an Antarctic ice floe, Shackleton and a few of his men endured an eight-hundred-mile trip across the frigid south Atlantic in little more than a rowboat to get help for his men. All twenty-seven men in the crew survived in good health.

Morrell and Capparell (2001, p. 45) list a few of Shackleton's leadership traits:

- Cultivate a sense of compassion and responsibility for others.

- Once you commit, stick through the tough learning period.

- Do your part to help create an upbeat environment at work—important for productivity.

- Broaden your cultural and social horizons, learning to see things from different perspectives.

- In a rapidly changing world, be willing to venture in new directions to seize new opportunities and learn new skills.

- Find a way to turn setbacks and failures to your own advantage.

- Be bold in vision and careful in planning.

- Learn from past mistakes.

- Never insist on reaching a goal at any cost; it must be achieved without undue hardship for your staff.

Sound familiar? Shackleton knew the six secrets; Scott didn't. The same incredibly ambitious goal was at stake, but was pursued from two very different leadership perspectives.

Aside from meaningful work and concern for peers, what are the other ingredients of happiness today? The best means to an answer comes from Jonathon Haidt (2006), who carefully picked his way to what he calls the "happiness hypothesis." He concludes that "happiness comes from between" (p. 213). It is neither only inside us nor only "out there." Happiness is, in other words, *relational*: it arises from our interactions with people and things in our environment. Once Haidt makes this key distinction—that happiness does not arise from the achievement of a given purpose, but from the sense of purpose itself—the question of what makes us happy becomes easier to understand.

The case for this theory of happiness is not an abstract, philosophical one. We can pose the question in empirical terms: What does evidence from the population at large tell us about happiness? Haidt finds that happiness derives from a combination of four elements: love (having meaningful attachments); meaningful work (which includes attachments, but also involves becoming more accomplished at what you are doing); vital engagement (the feeling you get when doing high-quality work that produces something of use to others); and cross-level coherence (when your sense of self physically and mentally meshes with the larger culture of which you are a part).

Haidt concludes, "The final version of the *Happiness Hypothesis* is that happiness comes from between. Happiness is not something you can find, acquire or achieve directly. You have to get the conditions right, and then wait. Some of these conditions are within you. Other conditions require relationships to things beyond you. . . . People need love, work, and a connection to something larger. It is worth striving to get the right relationships between yourself and others, between yourself and work, and between yourself and something larger than yourself. If you get these relationships right a sense of purpose will emerge" (pp. 238–239).

If you look closely, happiness as Haidt defines it overlaps with the six secrets. This book is about leadership, which means that you have a dual responsibility: to unlock the secrets for yourself, while at the same time creating the conditions for others to find happiness at work. Surviving and thriving, like happiness, does "come from between." Your work as a leader—including your interactions with others, both inside and outside the organization—can inspire happiness.

The six secrets give us a lot of food for thought. The reciprocal and synergistic relationships among them put successful action well within our reach. Because we can begin putting the secrets into practice without further study, they are immediately useful. The evidence across a range of situations tells us that people who employ the secrets gain more satisfaction and greater productivity, beginning a virtuous cycle in which the secrets become even more valuable.

The bottom line is, What is your purpose within life? My answer is that you will find your purpose by cultivating the six secrets. And you will contribute significantly to the welfare of others. Few things in life are more satisfying than the chance to share a good secret or six. Go for it.

# REFERENCES

Andersen, E. (2006). *Growing great employees: Turning ordinary people into extraordinary performers.* New York: Portfolio.

Barber, M. (2007). *Instruction to deliver.* London: Politico.

Barber, M., & Mourshed, M. (2007). *How the world's best-performing school systems come out on top.* London: McKinsey & Co.

Block, P. (1987). *The empowered manager.* San Francisco: Jossey-Bass.

Boudreau, J., & Ramstad, P. (2007). *Beyond HR: The new science of human capital.* Boston: Harvard Business School Press.

Charan, R. (2007). *Know-how: The eight skills that separate people who perform from those that don't.* New York: Crown.

Cohn, C. (2007). Empowering those at the bottom beats punishing them from the top. *Education Week, 26*(34), 32–33.

Cole, P. (2004). "Professional development: A great way to avoid change." Melbourne: Centre for Strategic Education.

Collier, P. (2007). *The bottom billion: Why the poorest countries are failing and what to do about it.* Oxford: Oxford University Press.

Collins, J. (2001). *Good to great.* New York: HarperCollins.

DeGues, A. (1997). *The living company.* Boston: Harvard Business School Press.

Ellis, C. (2006). *Joe Wilson and the creation of Xerox.* New York: Wiley.

Elmore, R. (2004). *School reform from the inside out.* Cambridge, MA: Harvard University Press.

Franceschini, L. (2002). *Memphis, what happened?* Paper presented at the American Education Research Association, New Orleans.

Frank, R. H. (1999). *Why money fails to satisfy in an era of success.* New York: Free Press.

Friedman, T. (2005). *The world is flat.* New York: Farrar, Straus & Giroux.

Fullan, M. (2001). *Leading in a culture of change.* San Francisco: Jossey-Bass.

Fullan, M. (2006). *Turnaround leadership.* San Francisco: Jossey-Bass.

Fullan, M. (2008). *What's worth fighting for in the principalship.* 2nd ed. New York: Teachers College Press (and Toronto: Ontario Principals' Council).

Fullan, M., Hill, P., & Crévola, C. (2006). *Breakthrough.* Thousand Oaks, CA: Corwin Press.

Gawande, A. (2007). *Better: A surgeon's notes on performance.* New York: Metropolitan Books.

Ghemawat, P. (2007). *Redefining global strategy.* Boston: Harvard Business School Press.

Gittell, J. (2003). *The Southwest Airlines way.* New York: McGraw-Hill.

Grnak, A., Hughes, J., & Hunter, P. D. (2006). *Building the best: Lessons from inside Canada's best managed companies.* Toronto: Viking.

Haidt, J. (2006). *The happiness hypothesis.* New York: Basic Books.

Hargreaves, A., & Fink, D. (2006). *Sustainable leadership.* San Francisco: Jossey-Bass.

Homer-Dixon, T. (2006). *The upside of down: Catastrophe, creativity and the renewal of civilization.* Toronto: Knopf.

How hectoring backfires. (2007, July 14). *Globe and Mail.*

Hubbard, L., Mehan, H., & Stein, M. K. (2006). *Reform as learning.* London: Routledge.

Is GE too big for its own good? (2007, July 22). *New York Times,* pp. B1–B2.

Janis, I. L. (1982). *Groupthink: Psychological studies of policy decisions and fiascoes.* Boston: Houghton-Mifflin.

Kanter, R. M. (2004). *Confidence: How winning and losing streaks begin and end.* New York: Crown Business.

Khurana, R. (2002). *Searching for a corporate savior: The irrational quest for charismatic CEOs.* Princeton, NJ: Princeton University Press.

Leithwood, K., Louis, K., Anderson, S., & Wahlstrom, K. (2004). *How leadership influences student learning.* New York: Wallace Foundation.

Lencioni, P. (2007). *The three signs of a miserable job.* San Francisco: Jossey-Bass.

Liker, J. (2004). *The Toyota way.* New York: McGraw-Hill.

Liker, J., & Meier, D. (2007). *Toyota talent.* New York: McGraw-Hill.

Martin, R. (2007). *The opposable mind.* Boston: Harvard Business School Press.

McGregor, D. (1960). *The human side of enterprise.* New York: McGraw-Hill.

McIntyre, F. (2006). *New teachers thriving by third year.* Toronto: Ontario College of Teachers.

McLean, B., & Elkind, P. (2003). *The smartest guys in the room: The amazing rise and scandalous fall of Enron.* New York: Portfolio.

Micklethwait, J., & Wooldridge, A. (1996). *The witch doctors: Making sense of management gurus.* New York: Times Business.

Miller, L. (2002). *Lincoln's virtues.* New York: Vintage Books.

Mintzberg, H. (2004). *Managers not MBAs.* San Francisco: Berrett-Koehler.

Morrell, M., & Capparell, S. (2001). *Shackleton's way.* New York: Viking Penguin.

New York City Department of Education. (2007). *Children first: A bold commonsense plan to create great schools.* New York: Author.

O'Toole, J. (1995). *The executive compass: Business and the good society.* Oxford: Oxford University Press.

Pfeffer, J. (2007). *What were they thinking? Unconventional wisdom about management.* Boston: Harvard Business School Press.

Pfeffer, J., & Sutton, R. I. (2000). *The knowing-doing gap: How smart companies turn knowledge into action.* Boston: Harvard Business School Press.

Pfeffer, J., & Sutton, R. I. (2006). *Hard facts, dangerous half-truths and total nonsense: Profiting from evidence-based management.* Boston: Harvard Business School Press.

Roberto, M. (2005). *Why great leaders don't take yes for an answer.* Boston: Harvard Business School Press.

Rosenzweig, P. (2007). *The halo effect and eight other business delusions that deceive managers.* New York: Free Press.

Rubin, R. (2003). *In an uncertain world.* New York: Random House.

Sartain, L., & Schumann, M. (2006). *Brand from the inside: Eight essentials to emotionally connect your employees to your business.* New York: Wiley.

Senge, P. (1990). *The fifth discipline.* New York: Doubleday.

Sheth, J. (2007). *The self-destructive habits of good companies.* Upper Saddle River, NJ: Wharton School Publishing.

Shirley, D., and Hargreaves, A. (2006). Data-driven to distraction. *Education Week, 26*(6), 32–33.

Sirota, D., Mischkind, L., & Meltzer, M. (2005). *The enthusiastic employee.* Upper Saddle River, NJ: Wharton School Publishing.

Sisodia, R., Wolfe, D., & Sheth, J. (2007). *Firms of endearment: How world-class companies profit from passion and purpose.* Upper Saddle River, NJ: Wharton School Publishing.

Sober, E., & Wilson, D. S. (1998). *Unto others: The evolution and psychology of unselfish behavior.* Cambridge, MA: Harvard University Press.

Surowiecki, J. (2004). *The wisdom of crowds.* New York: Random House.

Taylor, F. W. (2007). *The principles of scientific management.* Charleston, SC: Biblio Bazaar. (Original work published 1911)

Taylor, W., & LaBarre, P. (2006). *Mavericks at work: Why the most original minds in business win.* New York: Morrow.

Thornhill Secondary School. (2007). *Strengthening our literacy foundation*. Presentation to the Learning Fair. Toronto: York Region District School Board.

Welch, J. (2001). *Jack: Straight from the gut*. New York: Warner Business Books.

Welch, J., with Welch, S. (2005). *Winning*. New York: HarperCollins.

Wilkinson, R. (2005). *The impact of inequality*. London: New Press.

Wilson, D. S. (2007). *Evolution for everyone*. New York: Delacorte Press.

# INDEX

A
Accenture's Tiger Woods ads, 48–49, 53, 75, 96, 111, 117
Accountability: external, 102; internal, 124
Action learning, 5
Alvarado, T., 24
Andersen, E., 36
Anderson, S., 69

B
Bad habits of good companies, 15
Barber, M., 9, 10, 23, 66, 67, 95, 96, 103
Bersin, A., 24, 25
Blair, T., 9, 95
Block, P., 51
*The Bottom Billion,* 100, 114, 116
Boudreau, J., 4, 66

C
Capacity building: defined, 57; fear mongering versus, 60–63;

judgmentalism versus, 13, 58–60; as secret three, 11, 13; selection of talent, 64–71
Capparell, S., 36, 132, 133
CEO search process, 107–108. *See also* Leaders
Charan, R., 28
Chrysler, 28
Climate stress, 6, 112
Clinton, President, 116
Cohn, C., 25
Cole, P., 13, 86
Collier, P., 100, 103, 114, 115, 116, 129, 131
Collins, J., 7, 30
Complexity: respect for, 111–121; staying on far side of, 123, 130–131
Consistency and innovation, 76–86
Container Store, 29, 88
Costco, 29, 30, 31